ORESTEIA

AESCHYLUS

ORESTEIA

Translated by Richmond Lattimore

*Etchings by Elaine Raphael
and Don Bolognese*

.

A LIMITED EDITION

THE FRANKLIN LIBRARY
Franklin Center, Pennsylvania
1980

CONTENTS

ORESTEIA

AGAMEMNON

CHARACTERS

WATCHMAN

CLYTAEMESTRA

HERALD

AGAMEMNON

CASSANDRA

AEGISTHUS

CHORUS OF ARGIVE ELDERS

ATTENDANTS OF CLYTAEMESTRA: OF AGAMEMNON:
BODYGUARD OF AEGISTHUS
(ALL SILENT PARTS)

TIME, DIRECTLY AFTER THE FALL OF TROY.

AGAMEMNON

SCENE: *Argos, before the palace of King Agamemnon.*
The Watchman, who speaks the opening lines, is
posted on the roof of the palace. Clytaemestra's
entrances are made from a door in the center of the
stage; all others, from the wings.

[*The Watchman, alone.*]

I ask the gods some respite from the weariness
of this watchtime measured by years I lie awake
elbowed upon the Atreidae's roof dogwise to mark
the grand processionals of all the stars of night
burdened with winter and again with heat for men,
dynasties in their shining blazoned on the air,
these stars, upon their wane and when the rest arise.

I wait; to read the meaning in that beacon light,
a blaze of fire to carry out of Troy the rumor
and outcry of its capture; to such end a lady's
male strength of heart in its high confidence ordains.
Now as this bed stricken with night and drenched with
   dew
I keep, nor ever with kind dreams for company:
since fear in sleep's place stands forever at my head
against strong closure of my eyes, or any rest:
I mince such medicine against sleep failed: I sing,
only to weep again the pity of this house

no longer, as once, administered in the grand way.
Now let there be again redemption from distress,
the flare burning from the blackness in good augury.

[*A light shows in the distance.*]

Oh hail, blaze of the darkness, harbinger of day's
shining, and of processionals and dance and choirs
of multitudes in Argos for this day of grace.
Ahoy!
I cry the news aloud to Agamemnon's queen,
that she may rise up from her bed of state with speed
to raise the rumor of gladness welcoming this beacon,
and singing rise, if truly the citadel of Ilium
has fallen, as the shining of this flare proclaims.
I also, I, will make my choral prelude, since
my lord's dice cast aright are counted as my own,
and mine the tripled sixes of this torchlit throw.

May it only happen. May my king come home, and I
take up within this hand the hand I love. The rest
I leave to silence; for an ox stands huge upon
my tongue. The house itself, could it take voice, might
    speak
aloud and plain. I speak to those who understand,
but if they fail, I have forgotten everything.

[*Exit. The Chorus enters, speaking.*]

Ten years since the great contestants
of Priam's right,
Menelaus and Agamemnon, my lord,

twin throned, twin sceptered, in twofold power
of kings from God, the Atreidae,
put forth from this shore
the thousand ships of the Argives,
the strength and the armies.
Their cry of war went shrill from the heart,
as eagles stricken in agony
for young perished, high from the nest
eddy and circle
to bend and sweep of the wings' stroke,
lost far below
the fledgelings, the nest, and the tendance.
Yet someone hears in the air, a god,
Apollo, Pan, or Zeus, the high
thin wail of these sky-guests, and drives
late to its mark
the Fury upon the transgressors.

So drives Zeus the great guest god
the Atreidae against Alexander:
for one woman's promiscuous sake
the struggling masses, legs tired,
knees grinding in dust,
spears broken in the onset.
Danaans and Trojans
they have it alike. It goes as it goes
now. The end will be destiny.
You cannot burn flesh or pour unguents,
not innocent cool tears,
that will soften the gods' stiff anger.

But we; dishonored, old in our bones,
cast off even then from the gathering horde,
stay here, to prop up
on staves the strength of a baby.
Since the young vigor that urges
inward to the heart
is frail as age, no warcraft yet perfect,
while beyond age, leaf
withered, man goes three footed
no stronger than a child is,
a dream that falters in daylight.

> [*Clytaemestra enters quietly. The Chorus*
> *continues to speak.*]

But you, lady,
daughter of Tyndareus, Clytaemestra, our queen:
What is there to be done? What new thing have you
    heard?
In persuasion of what
report do you order such sacrifice?
To all the gods of the city,
the high and the deep spirits,
to them of the sky and the market places,
the altars blaze with oblations.
The staggered flame goes sky high
one place, then another,
drugged by the simple soft
persuasion of sacred unguents,
the deep stored oil of the kings.
Of these things what can be told
openly, speak.

Be healer to this perplexity
that grows now into darkness of thought,
while again sweet hope shining from the flames
beats back the pitiless pondering
of sorrow that eats my heart.

I have mastery yet to chant the wonder at the wayside
given to kings. Still by God's grace there surges within
    me
singing magic
grown to my life and power,
how the wild bird portent
hurled forth the Achaeans'
twin-stemmed power single hearted,
lords of the youth of Hellas,
with spear and hand of strength
to the land of Teucrus.
Kings of birds to the kings of the ships,
one black, one blazed with silver,
clear seen by the royal house
on the right, the spear hand,
they lighted, watched by all
tore a hare, ripe, bursting with young unborn yet,
stayed from her last fleet running.
Sing sorrow, sorrow: but good win out in the end.

Then the grave seer of the host saw through to the
    hearts divided,
knew the fighting sons of Atreus feeding on the hare
with the host, their people.

Seeing beyond, he spoke:
"With time, this foray
shall stalk the castle of Priam.
Before then, under
the walls, Fate shall spoil
in violence the rich herds of the people.
Only let no doom of the gods darken
upon this huge iron forged to curb Troy—
from inward. Artemis the undefiled
is angered with pity
at the flying hounds of her father
eating the unborn young in the hare and the shivering
    mother.
She is sick at the eagles' feasting.
Sing sorrow, sorrow: but good win out in the end.

Lovely you are and kind
to the tender young of ravening lions.
For sucklings of all the savage
beasts that lurk in the lonely places you have
    sympathy.
Grant meaning to these appearances
good, yet not without evil.
Healer Apollo, I pray you
let her not with crosswinds
bind the ships of the Danaans
to time-long anchorage
forcing a second sacrifice unholy, untasted,
working bitterness in the blood
and faith lost. For the terror returns like sickness to
    lurk in the house;

the secret anger remembers the child that shall be
   avenged."
Such, with great good things beside, rang out in the
   voice of Calchas,
these fatal signs from the birds by the way to the house
   of the princes,
wherewith in sympathy
sing sorrow, sorrow: but good win out in the end.

Zeus: whatever he may be, if this name
pleases him in invocation,
thus I call upon him.
I have pondered everything
yet I cannot find a way,
only Zeus, to cast this dead weight of ignorance
finally from out my brain.

He who in time long ago was great,
throbbing with gigantic strength,
shall be as if he never were, unspoken.
He who followed him has found
his master, and is gone.
Cry aloud without fear the victory of Zeus,
you will not have failed the truth:

Zeus, who guided men to think,
who has laid it down that wisdom
comes alone through suffering.
Still there drips in sleep against the heart
grief of memory; against
our pleasure we are temperate.

From the gods who sit in grandeur
grace comes somehow violent.

On that day the elder king
of the Achaean ships, no more
strict against the prophet's word,
turned with the crosswinds of fortune,
when no ship sailed, no pail was full,
and the Achaean people sulked
fast against the shore at Aulis
facing Chalcis, where the tides ebb and surge:

and winds blew from the Strymon, bearing
sick idleness, ships tied fast, and hunger,
distraction of the mind, carelessness
for hull and cable;
with time's length bent to double measure
by delay crumbled the flower and pride
of Argos. Then against the bitter wind
the seer's voice clashed out
another medicine
more hateful yet, and spoke of Artemis, so that the
    kings
dashed their staves to the ground and could not hold
    their tears.

The elder lord spoke aloud before them:
"My fate is angry if I disobey these,
but angry if I slaughter
this child, the beauty of my house,

with maiden blood shed staining
these father's hands beside the altar.
What of these things goes now without disaster?
How shall I fail my ships
and lose my faith of battle?
For them to urge such sacrifice of innocent blood
angrily, for their wrath is great—it is right. May all be
    well yet."

But when necessity's yoke was put upon him
he changed, and from the heart the breath came bitter
and sacrilegious, utterly infidel,
to warp a will now to be stopped at nothing.
The sickening in men's minds, tough,
reckless in fresh cruelty brings daring. He endured then
to sacrifice his daughter
to stay the strength of war waged for a woman,
first offering for the ships' sake.

Her supplications and her cries of father
were nothing, nor the child's lamentation
to kings passioned for battle.
The father prayed, called to his men to lift her
with strength of hand swept in her robes aloft
and prone above the altar, as you might lift
a goat for sacrifice, with guards
against the lips' sweet edge, to check
the curse cried on the house of Atreus
by force of bit and speech drowned in strength.

Pouring then to the ground her saffron mantle
she struck the sacrificers with
the eyes' arrows of pity,
lovely as in a painted scene, and striving
to speak—as many times
at the kind festive table of her father
she had sung, and in the clear voice of a stainless
    maiden
with love had graced the song
of worship when the third cup was poured.

What happened next I saw not, neither speak it.
The crafts of Calchas fail not of outcome.
Justice so moves that those only learn
who suffer; and the future
you shall know when it has come; before then, forget
    it.
It is grief too soon given.
All will come clear in the next dawn's sunlight.
Let good fortune follow these things as
she who is here desires,
our Apian land's singlehearted protectress.

> [*The Chorus now turns toward Clytaemestra,*
> *and the leader speaks to her.*]

I have come in reverence, Clytaemestra, of your power.
For when the man is gone and the throne void, his right
falls to the prince's lady, and honor must be given.
Is it some grace—or otherwise—that you have heard

to make you sacrifice at messages of good hope?
I should be glad to hear, but must not blame your
   silence.

CLYTAEMESTRA

As it was said of old, may the dawn child be born
to be an angel of blessing from the kindly night.
You shall know joy beyond all you ever hoped to hear.
The men of Argos have taken Priam's citadel.

CHORUS

What have you said? Your words escaped my unbelief.

CLYTAEMESTRA

The Achaeans are in Troy. Is that not clear enough?

CHORUS

This slow delight steals over me to bring forth tears.

CLYTAEMESTRA

Yes, for your eyes betray the loyal heart within.

CHORUS

Yet how can I be certain? Is there some evidence?

CLYTAEMESTRA

There is, there must be; unless a god has lied to me.

CHORUS

Is it dream visions, easy to believe, you credit?

CLYTAEMESTRA

I accept nothing from a brain that is dull with sleep.

CHORUS

The charm, then, of some rumor, that made rich your
hope?

CLYTAEMESTRA

Am I some young girl, that you find my thoughts so
silly?

CHORUS

How long, then, is it since the citadel was stormed?

CLYTAEMESTRA

It is the night, the mother of this dawn I hailed.

CHORUS

What kind of messenger could come in speed like this?

CLYTAEMESTRA

Hephaestus, who cast forth the shining blaze from Ida.
And beacon after beacon picking up the flare
carried it here; Ida to the Hermaean horn
of Lemnos, where it shone above the isle, and next
the sheer rock face of Zeus on Athos caught it up;
and plunging skyward to arch the shoulders of the sea
the strength of the running flare in exultation,
pine timbers flaming into gold, like the sunrise,
brought the bright message to Macistus' sentinel cliffs,
who, never slow nor in the carelessness of sleep
caught up, sent on his relay in the courier chain,
and far across Euripus' streams the beacon flare
carried to signal watchmen on Messapion.

These took it again in turn, and heaping high a pile
of silvery brush flamed it to throw the message on.
And the flare sickened never, but grown stronger yet
outleapt the river valley of Asopus like
the very moon for shining, to Cithaeron's scaur
to waken the next station of the flaming post.
These watchers, not contemptuous of the far-thrown
blaze,
kindled another beacon vaster than commanded.
The light leaned high above Gorgopis' staring marsh,
and striking Aegyplanctus' mountain top, drove on
yet one more relay, lest the flare die down in speed.
Kindled once more with stintless heaping force, they
send
the beard of flame to hugeness, passing far beyond
the promontory that gazes on the Saronic strait
and flaming far, until it plunged at last to strike
the steep rock of Arachnus near at hand, our
watchtower.
And thence there fell upon this house of Atreus' sons
the flare whose fathers mount to the Idaean beacon.
These are the changes on my torchlight messengers,
one from another running out the laps assigned.
The first and the last sprinters have the victory.
By such proof and such symbol I announce to you
my lord at Troy has sent his messengers to me.

CHORUS

The gods, lady, shall have my prayers and thanks
straightway.

And yet to hear your story till all wonder fades
would be my wish, could you but tell it once again.

CLYTAEMESTRA

The Achaeans have got Troy, upon this very day.
I think the city echoes with a clash of cries.
Pour vinegar and oil into the selfsame bowl,
you could not say they mix in friendship, but fight on.
Thus variant sound the voices of the conquerors
and conquered, from the opposition of their fates.
Trojans are stooping now to gather in their arms
their dead, husbands and brothers; children lean to
    clasp
the aged who begot them, crying upon the death
of those most dear, from lips that never will be free.
The Achaeans have their midnight work after the
    fighting
that sets them down to feed on all the city has,
ravenous, headlong, by no rank and file assigned,
but as each man has drawn his shaken lot by chance.
And in the Trojan houses that their spears have taken
they settle now, free of the open sky, the frosts
and dampness of the evening; without sentinels set
they sleep the sleep of happiness the whole night
    through.
And if they reverence the gods who hold the city
and all the holy temples of the captured land,
they, the despoilers, might not be despoiled in turn.
Let not their passion overwhelm them; let no lust
seize on these men to violate what they must not.

The run to safety and home is yet to make; they must
turn
the pole, and run the backstretch of the double course.
Yet though the host come home without offence to
high
gods, even so the anger of these slaughtered men
may never sleep. Oh, let there be no fresh wrong done!

Such are the thoughts you hear from me, a woman
merely.
Yet may the best win through, that none may fail to
see.
Of all good things to wish this is my dearest choice.

CHORUS

My lady, no grave man could speak with better grace.
I have listened to the proofs of your tale, and I believe,
and go to make my glad thanksgivings to the gods.
This pleasure is not unworthy of the grief that gave it.
O Zeus our lord and Night beloved,
bestower of power and beauty,
you slung above the bastions of Troy
the binding net, that none, neither great
nor young, might outleap
the gigantic toils
of enslavement and final disaster.
I gaze in awe on Zeus of the guests
who wrung from Alexander such payment.
He bent the bow with slow care, that neither
the shaft might hurdle the stars, nor fall

spent to the earth, short driven.
They have the stroke of Zeus to tell of.
This thing is clear and you may trace it.
He acted as he had decreed. A man thought
the gods deigned not to punish mortals
who trampled down the delicacy of things
inviolable. That man was wicked.
The curse on great daring
shines clear; it wrings atonement
from those high hearts that drive to evil,
from houses blossoming to pride
and peril. Let there be
wealth without tears; enough for
the wise man who will ask no further.
There is not any armor
in gold against perdition
for him who spurns the high altar
of Justice down to the darkness.

Persuasion the persistent overwhelms him,
she, strong daughter of designing Ruin.
And every medicine is vain; the sin
smolders not, but burns to evil beauty.
As cheap bronze tortured
at the touchstone relapses
to blackness and grime, so this man
tested shows vain
as a child that strives to catch the bird flying
and wins shame that shall bring down his city.
No god will hear such a man's entreaty,

but whoso turns to these ways
they strike him down in his wickedness.
This was Paris: he came
to the house of the sons of Atreus,
stole the woman away, and shamed
the guest's right of the board shared.

She left among her people the stir and clamor
of shields and of spearheads,
the ships to sail and the armor.
She took to Ilium her dowry, death.
She stepped forth lightly between the gates
daring beyond all daring. And the prophets
about the great house wept aloud and spoke:
"Alas, alas for the house and for the champions,
alas for the bed signed with their love together.
Here now is silence, scorned, unreproachful.
The agony of his loss is clear before us.
Longing for her who lies beyond the sea
he shall see a phantom queen in his household.
Her images in their beauty
are bitterness to her lord now
where in the emptiness of eyes
all passion has faded."

Shining in dreams the sorrowful
memories pass; they bring him
vain delight only.
It is vain, to dream and to see splendors,
and the image slipping from the arms' embrace

escapes, not to return again,
on wings drifting down the ways of sleep.
Such have the sorrows been in the house by the
hearthside;
such have there been, and yet there are worse than these.
In all Hellas, for those who swarmed to the host
the heartbreaking misery
shows in the house of each.
Many are they who are touched at the heart by these
things.
Those they sent forth they knew;
now, in place of the young men
urns and ashes are carried home
to the houses of the fighters.

The god of war, money changer of dead bodies,
held the balance of his spear in the fighting,
and from the corpse-fires at Ilium
sent to their dearest the dust
heavy and bitter with tears shed
packing smooth the urns with
ashes that once were men.
They praise them through their tears, how this man
knew well the craft of battle, how another
went down splendid in the slaughter:
and all for some strange woman.
Thus they mutter in secrecy,
and the slow anger creeps below their grief
at Atreus' sons and their quarrels.
There by the walls of Ilium

the young men in their beauty keep
graves deep in the alien soil
they hated and they conquered.

The citizens speak: their voice is dull with hatred.
The curse of the people must be paid for.
There lurks for me in the hooded night
terror of what may be told me.
The gods fail not to mark
those who have killed many.
The black Furies stalking the man
fortunate beyond all right
wrench back again the set of his life
and drop him to darkness. There among
the ciphers there is no more comfort
in power. And the vaunt of high glory
is bitterness; for God's thunderbolts
crash on the towering mountains.
Let me attain no envied wealth,
let me not plunder cities,
neither be taken in turn, and face
life in the power of another.

[*Various members of the Chorus, speaking
severally.*]

From the beacon's bright message
the fleet rumor runs
through the city. If this be real
who knows? Perhaps the gods have sent some lie to us.

AGAMEMNON · 21

Who of us is so childish or so reft of wit
that by the beacon's messages
his heart flamed must despond again
when the tale changes in the end?

It is like a woman indeed
to take the rapture before the fact has shown for true.

They believe too easily, are too quick to shift
from ground to ground; and swift indeed
the rumor voiced by a woman dies again.

Now we shall understand these torches and their
    shining,
the beacons, and the interchange of flame and flame.
They may be real; yet bright and dreamwise ecstasy
in light's appearance might have charmed our hearts
    awry.
I see a herald coming from the beach, his brows
shaded with sprigs of olive; and upon his feet
the dust, dry sister of the mire, makes plain to me
that he will find a voice, not merely kindle flame
from mountain timber, and make signals from the
    smoke,
but tell us outright, whether to be happy, or—
but I shrink back from naming the alternative.
That which appeared was good; may yet more good be
    given.

And any man who prays that different things befall
the city, may he reap the crime of his own heart.

[*The Herald enters, and speaks.*]

Soil of my fathers, Argive earth I tread upon,
in daylight of the tenth year I have come back to you.
All my hopes broke but one, and this I have at last.
I never could have dared to dream that I might die
in Argos, and be buried in this beloved soil.
Hail to the Argive land and to its sunlight, hail
to its high sovereign, Zeus, and to the Pythian king.
May you no longer shower your arrows on our heads.
Beside Scamandrus you were grim; be satisfied
and turn to savior now and healer of our hurts,
my lord Apollo. Gods of the market place assembled,
I greet you all, and my own patron deity
Hermes, beloved herald, in whose right all heralds
are sacred; and you heroes that sent forth the host,
propitiously take back all that the spear has left.
O great hall of the kings and house beloved; seats
of sanctity; divinities that face the sun:
if ever before, look now with kind and glowing eyes
to greet our king in state after so long a time.
He comes, lord Agamemnon, bearing light in gloom
to you, and to all that are assembled here.
Salute him with good favor, as he well deserves,
the man who has wrecked Ilium with the spade of Zeus
vindictive, whereby all their plain has been laid waste.
Gone are their altars, the sacred places of the gods
are gone, and scattered all the seed within the ground.
With such a yoke as this gripped to the neck of Troy
he comes, the king, Atreus' elder son, a man
fortunate to be honored far above all men
alive; not Paris nor the city tied to him
can boast he did more than was done him in return.

Guilty of rape and theft, condemned, he lost the prize
captured, and broke to sheer destruction all the house
of his fathers, with the very ground whereon it stood.
Twice over the sons of Priam have atoned their sins.

CHORUS

Hail and be glad, herald of the Achaean host.

HERALD

I am happy; I no longer ask the gods for death.

CHORUS

Did passion for your country so strip bare your heart?

HERALD

So that the tears broke in my eyes, for happiness.

CHORUS

You were taken with that sickness, then, that brings
delight.

HERALD

How? I cannot deal with such words until I understand.

CHORUS

Struck with desire of those who loved as much again.

HERALD

You mean our country longed for us, as we for home?

CHORUS

So that I sighed, out of the darkness of my heart.

HERALD

Whence came this black thought to afflict the mind
with fear?

CHORUS

Long since it was my silence kept disaster off.

HERALD

But how? There were some you feared when the kings
went away?

CHORUS

So much that as you said now, even death were grace.

HERALD

Well: the end has been good. And in the length of time
part of our fortune you could say held favorable,
but part we cursed again. And who, except the gods,
can live time through forever without any pain?
Were I to tell you of the hard work done, the nights
exposed, the cramped sea-quarters, the foul beds—what
   part
of day's disposal did we not cry out loud?
Ashore, the horror stayed with us and grew. We lay
against the ramparts of our enemies, and from
the sky, and from the ground, the meadow dews came
   out
to soak our clothes and fill our hair with lice. And if
I were to tell of winter time, when all birds died,

the snows of Ida past endurance she sent down,
or summer heat, when in the lazy noon the sea
fell level and asleep under a windless sky—
but why live such grief over again? That time is gone
for us, and gone for those who died. Never again
need they rise up, nor care again for anything.
Why must a live man count the numbers of the slain,
why grieve at fortune's wrath that fades to break once
    more?
I call a long farewell to all our unhappiness.
For us, survivors of the Argive armament,
the pleasure wins, pain casts no weight in the opposite
    scale.
And here, in this sun's shining, we can boast aloud,
whose fame has gone with wings across the land and
    sea:
"Upon a time the Argive host took Troy, and on
the houses of the gods who live in Hellas nailed
the spoils, to be the glory of days long ago."
And they who hear such things shall call this city blest
and the leaders of the host; and high the grace of God
shall be exalted, that did this. You have the story.

CHORUS

I must give way; your story shows that I was wrong.
Old men are always young enough to learn, with profit.
But Clytaemestra and her house must hear, above
others, this news that makes luxurious my life.

[*Clytaemestra comes forward and speaks.*]

I raised my cry of joy, and it was long ago
when the first beacon flare of message came by night
to speak of capture and of Ilium's overthrow.
But there was one who laughed at me, who said: "You trust
in beacons so, and you believe that Troy has fallen?
How like a woman, for the heart to lift so light."
Men spoke like that; they thought I wandered in my wits;
yet I made sacrifice, and in the womanish strain
voice after voice caught up the cry along the city
to echo in the temples of the gods and bless
and still the fragrant flame that melts the sacrifice.

Why should you tell me then the whole long tale at large
when from my lord himself I shall hear all the story?
But now, how best to speed my preparation to
receive my honored lord come home again—what else
is light more sweet for woman to behold than this,
to spread the gates before her husband home from war
and saved by God's hand?—take this message to the king:
Come, and with speed, back to the city that longs for him,
and may he find a wife within his house as true
as on the day he left her, watchdog of the house
gentle to him alone, fierce to his enemies,
and such a woman in all her ways as this, who has

not broken the seal upon her in the length of days.
With no man else have I known delight, nor any shame
of evil speech, more than I know how to temper bronze.

[Clytaemestra goes to the back of the stage.]

HERALD

A vaunt like this, so loaded as it is with truth,
it well becomes a highborn lady to proclaim.

CHORUS

Thus has she spoken to you, and well you understand,
words that impress interpreters whose thought is clear.
But tell me, herald; I would learn of Menelaus,
that power beloved in this land. Has he survived
also, and come with you back to his home again?

HERALD

I know no way to lie and make my tale so fair
that friends could reap joy of it for any length of time.

CHORUS

Is there no means to speak us fair, and yet tell the
truth?
It will not hide, when truth and good are torn asunder.

HERALD

He is gone out of the sight of the Achaean host,
vessel and man alike. I speak no falsehood there.

CHORUS

Was it when he had put out from Ilium in your sight,
or did a storm that struck you both whirl him away?

HERALD

How like a master bowman you have hit the mark
and in your speech cut a long sorrow to brief stature.

CHORUS

But then the rumor in the host that sailed beside,
was it that he had perished, or might yet be living?

HERALD

No man knows. There is none could tell us that for
sure
except the Sun, from whom this earth has life and
increase.

CHORUS

How did this storm, by wrath of the divinities,
strike on our multitude at sea? How did it end?

HERALD

It is not well to stain the blessing of this day
with speech of evil weight. Such gods are honored
apart.
And when the messenger of a shaken host, sad faced,
brings to his city news it prayed never to hear,
this scores one wound upon the body of the people;
and that from many houses many men are slain
by the two-lashed whip dear to the War God's hand,
this turns
disaster double-bladed, bloodily made two.
The messenger so freighted with a charge of tears
should make his song of triumph at the Furies' door.

But, carrying the fair message of our hopes' salvation,
come home to a glad city's hospitality,
how shall I mix my gracious news with foul, and tell
of the storm on the Achaeans by God's anger sent?
For they, of old the deepest enemies, sea and fire,
made a conspiracy and gave the oath of hand
to blast in ruin our unhappy Argive army.
At night the sea began to rise in waves of death.
Ship against ship the Thracian stormwind shattered us,
and gored and split, our vessels, swept in violence
of storm and whirlwind, beaten by the breaking rain,
drove on in darkness, spun by the wicked shepherd's
    hand.
But when the sun came up again to light the dawn,
we saw the Aegaean Sea blossoming with dead men,
the men of Achaea, and the wreckage of their ships.
For us, and for our ship, some god, no man, by guile
or by entreaty's force prevailing, laid his hand
upon the helm and brought us through with hull
    unscarred.
Life-giving fortune deigned to take our ship in charge
that neither riding in deep water she took the surf
nor drove to shoal and break upon some rocky shore.
But then, delivered from death at sea, in the pale day,
incredulous of our own luck, we shepherded
in our sad thoughts the fresh disaster of the fleet
so pitifully torn and shaken by the storm.
Now of these others, if there are any left alive
they speak of us as men who perished, must they not?

Even as we, who fear that they are gone. But may
it all come well in the end. For Menelaus: be sure
if any of them come back that he will be the first.
If he is still where some sun's gleam can track him
    down,
alive and open-eyed, by blessed hand of God
who willed that not yet should his seed be utterly gone,
there is some hope that he will still come home again.
You have heard all; and be sure, you have heard the
    truth.

[*The Herald goes out.*]

CHORUS

Who is he that named you so
fatally in every way?
Could it be some mind unseen
in divination of your destiny
shaping to the lips that name
for the bride of spears and blood,
Helen, which is death? Appropriately
death of ships, death of men and cities
from the bower's soft curtained
and secluded luxury she sailed then,
driven on the giant west wind,
and armored men in their thousands came,
huntsmen down the oar blade's fading footprint
to struggle in blood with those
who by the banks of Simoeis
beached their hulls where the leaves break.

And on Ilium in truth
in the likeness of the name
the sure purpose of the Wrath drove
marriage with death: for the guest board
shamed, and Zeus kindly to strangers,
the vengeance wrought on those men
who graced in too loud voice the bride-song
fallen to their lot to sing,
the kinsmen and the brothers.
And changing its song's measure
the ancient city of Priam
chants in high strain of lamentation,
calling Paris him of the fatal marriage;
for it endured its life's end
in desolation and tears
and the piteous blood of its people.

Once a man fostered in his house
a lion cub, from the mother's milk
torn, craving the breast given.
In the first steps of its young life
mild, it played with children
and delighted the old.
Caught in the arm's cradle
they pampered it like a newborn child,
shining eyed and broken to the hand
to stay the stress of its hunger.

But it grew with time, and the lion
in the blood strain came out; it paid

grace to those who had fostered it
in blood and death for the sheep flocks,
a grim feast forbidden.
The house reeked with blood run
nor could its people beat down the bane,
the giant murderer's onslaught.
This thing they raised in their house was blessed
by God to be priest of destruction.

And that which first came to the city of Ilium,
call it a dream of calm
and the wind dying,
the loveliness and luxury of much gold,
the melting shafts of the eyes' glances,
the blossom that breaks the heart with longing.
But she turned in mid-step of her course to make
bitter the consummation,
whirling on Priam's people
to blight with her touch and nearness.
Zeus hospitable sent her,
a vengeance to make brides weep.

It has been made long since and grown old among men,
this saying: human wealth
grown to fulness of stature
breeds again nor dies without issue.
From high good fortune in the blood
blossoms the quenchless agony.
Far from others I hold my own
mind; only the act of evil

breeds others to follow,
young sins in its own likeness.
Houses clear in their right are given
children in all loveliness.

But Pride aging is made
in men's dark actions
ripe with the young pride
late or soon when the dawn of destiny
comes and birth is given
to the spirit none may fight nor beat down,
sinful Daring; and in those halls
the black visaged Disasters stamped
in the likeness of their fathers.

And Righteousness is a shining in
the smoke of mean houses.
Her blessing is on the just man.
From high halls starred with gold by reeking hands
she turns back
with eyes that glance away to the simple in heart,
spurning the strength of gold
stamped false with flattery.
And all things she steers to fulfilment.

> [*Agamemnon enters in a chariot, with
> Cassandra beside him. The Chorus speaks
> to him.*]

Behold, my king: sacker of Troy's citadel,
own issue of Atreus.
How shall I hail you? How give honor

not crossing too high nor yet bending short
of this time's graces?
For many among men are they who set high
the show of honor, yet break justice.
If one be unhappy, all else are fain
to grieve with him: yet the teeth of sorrow
come nowise near to the heart's edge.
And in joy likewise they show joy's semblance,
and torture the face to the false smile.
Yet the good shepherd, who knows his flock,
the eyes of men cannot lie to him,
that with water of feigned
love seem to smile from the true heart.
But I: when you marshalled this armament
for Helen's sake, I will not hide it,
in ugly style you were written in my heart
for steering aslant the mind's course
to bring home by blood
sacrifice and dead men that wild spirit.
But now, in love drawn up from the deep heart,
not skimmed at the edge, we hail you.
You have won, your labor is made gladness.
Ask all men: you will learn in time
which of your citizens have been just
in the city's sway, which were reckless.

AGAMEMNON

To Argos first, and to the gods within the land,
I must give due greeting; they have worked with me to
  bring

me home; they helped me in the vengeance I have
   wrought
on Priam's city. Not from the lips of men the gods
heard justice, but in one firm cast they laid their votes
within the urn of blood that Ilium must die
and all her people; while above the opposite vase
the hand hovered and there was hope, but no vote fell.
The stormclouds of their ruin live; the ash that dies
upon them gushes still in smoke their pride of wealth.
For all this we must thank the gods with grace of much
high praise and memory, we who fenced within our
   toils
of wrath the city; and, because one woman strayed,
the beast of Argos broke them, the fierce young within
the horse, the armored people who marked out their
   leap
against the setting of the Pleiades. A wild
and bloody lion swarmed above the towers of Troy
to glut its hunger lapping at the blood of kings.

This to the gods, a prelude strung to length of words.
But, for the thought you spoke, I heard and I remember
and stand behind you. For I say that it is true.
In few men is it part of nature to respect
a friend's prosperity without begrudging him,
as envy's wicked poison settling to the heart
piles up the pain in one sick with unhappiness,
who, staggered under sufferings that are all his own,
winces again to the vision of a neighbor's bliss.
And I can speak, for I have seen, I know it well,

this mirror of companionship, this shadow's ghost,
these men who seemed my friends in all sincerity.
One man of them all, Odysseus, he who sailed
    unwilling,
once yoked to me carried his harness, nor went slack.
Dead though he be or living, I can say it still.

Now in the business of the city and the gods
we must ordain full conclave of all citizens
and take our counsel. We shall see what element
is strong, and plan that it shall keep its virtue still.
But that which must be healed—we must use
    medicine,
or burn, or amputate, with kind intention, take
all means at hand that might beat down corruption's
    pain.
So to the King's house and the home about the hearth
I take my way, with greeting to the gods within
who sent me forth, and who have brought me home
    once more.
My prize was conquest; may it never fail again.

                [*Clytaemestra comes forward and speaks.*]
Grave gentlemen of Argolis assembled here,
I take no shame to speak aloud before you all
the love I bear my husband. In the lapse of time
modesty fades; it is human.
                            What I tell you now
I learned not from another; this is my own sad life
all the long years this man was gone at Ilium.

It is evil and a thing of terror when a wife
sits in the house forlorn with no man by, and hears
rumors that like a fever die to break again,
and men come in with news of fear, and on their heels
another messenger, with worse news to cry aloud
here in this house. Had Agamemnon taken all
the wounds the tale whereof was carried home to me,
he had been cut full of gashes like a fishing net.
If he had died each time that rumor told his death,
he must have been some triple-bodied Geryon
back from the dead with threefold cloak of earth upon
his body, and killed once for every shape assumed.
Because such tales broke out forever on my rest,
many a time they cut me down and freed my throat
from the noose overslung where I had caught it fast.
And therefore is your son, in whom my love and yours
are sealed and pledged, not here to stand with us today,
Orestes. It were right; yet do not be amazed.
Strophius of Phocis, comrade in arms and faithful friend
to you, is keeping him. He spoke to me of peril
on two counts; of your danger under Ilium,
and here, of revolution and the clamorous people
who might cast down the council—since it lies in
    men's
nature to trample on the fighter already down.
Such my excuse to you, and without subterfuge.

For me: the rippling springs that were my tears have
    dried
utterly up, nor left one drop within. I keep
the pain upon my eyes where late at night I wept

over the beacons long ago set for your sake,
untended left forever. In the midst of dreams
the whisper that a gnat's thin wings could winnow
   broke
my sleep apart. I thought I saw you suffer wounds
more than the time that slept with me could ever hold.

Now all my suffering is past, with griefless heart
I hail this man, the watchdog of the fold and hall;
the stay that keeps the ship alive; the post to grip
groundward the towering roof; a father's single child;
land seen by sailors after all their hope was gone;
splendor of daybreak shining from the night of storm;
the running spring a parched wayfarer strays upon.
Oh, it is sweet to escape from all necessity!

Such is my greeting to him, that he well deserves.
Let none bear malice; for the harm that went before
I took, and it was great.
                              Now, my beloved one,
step from your chariot; yet let not your foot, my lord,
sacker of Ilium, touch the earth. My maidens there!
Why this delay? Your task has been appointed you,
to strew the ground before his feet with tapestries.
Let there spring up into the house he never hoped
to see, where Justice leads him in, a crimson path.

In all things else, my heart's unsleeping care shall act
with the gods' aid to set aright what fate ordained.

*[Clytaemestra's handmaidens spread a bright
carpet between the chariot and the door.]*

AGAMEMNON

Daughter of Leda, you who kept my house for me,
there is one way your welcome matched my absence
   well.
You strained it to great length. Yet properly to praise
me thus belongs by right to other lips, not yours.
And all this—do not try in woman's ways to make
me delicate, nor, as if I were some Asiatic
bow down to earth and with wide mouth cry out to me,
nor cross my path with jealousy by strewing the ground
with robes. Such state becomes the gods, and none
   beside.
I am a mortal, a man; I cannot trample upon
these tinted splendors without fear thrown in my path.
I tell you, as a man, not god, to reverence me.
Discordant is the murmur at such treading down
of lovely things; while God's most lordly gift to man
is decency of mind. Call that man only blest
who has in sweet tranquillity brought his life to close.
If I could only act as such, my hope is good.

CLYTAEMESTRA

Yet tell me this one thing, and do not cross my will.

AGAMEMNON

My will is mine. I shall not make it soft for you.

CLYTAEMESTRA

It was in fear surely that you vowed this course to God.

AGAMEMNON

No man has spoken knowing better what he said.

CLYTAEMESTRA

If Priam had won as you have, what would he have done?

AGAMEMNON

I well believe he might have walked on tapestries.

CLYTAEMESTRA

Be not ashamed before the bitterness of men.

AGAMEMNON

The people murmur, and their voice is great in strength.

CLYTAEMESTRA

Yet he who goes unenvied shall not be admired.

AGAMEMNON

Surely this lust for conflict is not womanlike?

CLYTAEMESTRA

Yet for the mighty even to give way is grace.

AGAMEMNON

Does such a victory as this mean so much to you?

CLYTAEMESTRA

Oh yield! The power is yours. Give way of your free will.

AGAMEMNON

Since you must have it—here, let someone with all speed
take off these sandals, slaves for my feet to tread upon.

And as I crush these garments stained from the rich sea
let no god's eyes of hatred strike me from afar.
Great the extravagance, and great the shame I feel
to spoil such treasure and such silver's worth of webs.

So much for all this. Take this stranger girl within
now, and be kind. The conqueror who uses softly
his power, is watched from far in the kind eyes of God,
and this slave's yoke is one no man will wear from
    choice.
Gift of the host to me, and flower exquisite
from all my many treasures, she attends me here.

Now since my will was bent to listen to you in this
my feet crush purple as I pass within the hall.

CLYTAEMESTRA

The sea is there, and who shall drain its yield? It breeds
precious as silver, ever of itself renewed,
the purple ooze wherein our garments shall be dipped.
And by God's grace this house keeps full sufficiency
of all. Poverty is a thing beyond its thought.
I could have vowed to trample many splendors down
had such decree been ordained from the oracles
those days when all my study was to bring home your
    life.
For when the root lives yet the leaves will come again
to fence the house with shade against the Dog Star's
    heat,
and now you have come home to keep your hearth and
    house

you bring with you the symbol of our winter's warmth;
but when Zeus ripens the green clusters into wine
there shall be coolness in the house upon those days
because the master ranges his own halls once more.

Zeus, Zeus accomplisher, accomplish these my prayers.
Let your mind bring these things to pass. It is your will.

> [*Agamemnon and Clytaemestra enter the*
> *house. Cassandra remains in the chariot. The*
> *Chorus speaks.*]

Why must this persistent fear
beat its wings so ceaselessly
and so close against my mantic heart?
Why this strain unwanted, unrepaid, thus prophetic?
Nor can valor of good hope
seated near the chambered depth
of the spirit cast it out
as dreams of dark fancy; and yet time
has buried in the mounding sand
the sea cables since that day
when against Ilium
the army and the ships put to sea.

Yet I have seen with these eyes
Agamemnon home again.
Still the spirit sings, drawing deep
from within this unlyric threnody of the Fury.
Hope is gone utterly,
the sweet strength is far away.

Surely this is not fantasy.
Surely it is real, this whirl of drifts
that spin the stricken heart.
Still I pray; may all this
expectation fade as vanity
into unfulfilment, and not be.

Yet it is true: the high strength of men
knows no content with limitation. Sickness
chambered beside it beats at the wall between.
Man's fate that sets a true
course yet may strike upon
the blind and sudden reefs of disaster.
But if before such time, fear
throw overboard some precious thing
of the cargo, with deliberate cast,
not all the house, laboring
with weight of ruin, shall go down,
nor sink the hull deep within the sea.
And great and affluent the gift of Zeus
in yield of ploughed acres year on year
makes void again sick starvation.

But when the black and mortal blood of man
has fallen to the ground before his feet, who then
can sing spells to call it back again?
Did Zeus not warn us once
when he struck to impotence
that one who could in truth charm back the dead men?
Had the gods not so ordained

that fate should stand against fate
to check any man's excess,
my heart now would have outrun speech
to break forth the water of its grief.
But this is so; I murmur deep in darkness
sore at heart; my hope is gone now
ever again to unwind some crucial good
from the flames about my heart.

[*Clytaemestra comes out from the house
again and speaks to Cassandra.*]

Cassandra, you may go within the house as well,
since Zeus in no unkindness has ordained that you
must share our lustral water, stand with the great
    throng
of slaves that flock to the altar of our household god.
Step from this chariot, then, and do not be so proud.
And think—they say that long ago Alcmena's son
was sold in bondage and endured the bread of slaves.
But if constraint of fact forces you to such fate,
be glad indeed for masters ancient in their wealth.
They who have reaped success beyond their dreams of
    hope
are savage above need and standard toward their slaves.
From us you shall have all you have the right to ask.

CHORUS

What she has spoken is for you, and clear enough.
Fenced in these fatal nets wherein you find yourself
you should obey her if you can; perhaps you can not.

CLYTAEMESTRA

Unless she uses speech incomprehensible,
barbarian, wild as the swallow's song, I speak
within her understanding, and she must obey.

CHORUS

Go with her. What she bids is best in circumstance
that rings you now. Obey, and leave this carriage seat.

CLYTAEMESTRA

I have no leisure to stand outside the house and waste
time on this woman. At the central altarstone
the flocks are standing, ready for the sacrifice
we make to this glad day we never hoped to see.
You: if you are obeying my commands at all, be quick.
But if in ignorance you fail to comprehend,
speak not, but make with your barbarian hand some
    sign.

CHORUS

I think this stranger girl needs some interpreter
who understands. She is like some captive animal.

CLYTAEMESTRA

No, she is in the passion of her own wild thoughts.
Leaving her captured city she has come to us
untrained to take the curb, and will not understand
until her rage and strength have foamed away in blood.
I shall throw down no more commands for her
    contempt.

[*Clytaemestra goes back into the house.*]

CHORUS

I, though, shall not be angry, for I pity her.
Come down, poor creature, leave the empty car. Give
  way
to compulsion and take up the yoke that shall be yours.

*[Cassandra descends from the chariot and
cries out loud.]*

Oh shame upon the earth!
Apollo, Apollo!

CHORUS

You cry on Loxias in agony? He is not
of those immortals the unhappy supplicate.

CASSANDRA

Oh shame upon the earth!
Apollo, Apollo!

CHORUS

Now once again in bitter voice she calls upon
this god, who has not part in any lamentation.

CASSANDRA

Apollo, Apollo!
Lord of the ways, my ruin.
You have undone me once again, and utterly.

CHORUS

I think she will be prophetic of her own disaster.
Even in the slave's heart the gift divine lives on.

CASSANDRA

Apollo, Apollo!
Lord of the ways, my ruin.
Where have you led me now at last? What house is
    this?

CHORUS

The house of the Atreidae. If you understand
not that, I can tell you; and so much at least is true.

CASSANDRA

No, but a house that God hates, guilty within
of kindred blood shed, torture of its own,
the shambles for men's butchery, the dripping floor.

CHORUS

The stranger is keen scented like some hound upon
the trail of blood that leads her to discovered death.

CASSANDRA

Behold there the witnesses to my faith.
The small children wail for their own death
and the flesh roasted that their father fed upon.

CHORUS

We had been told before of this prophetic fame
of yours: we want no prophets in this place at all.

CASSANDRA

Ah, for shame, what can she purpose now?
What is this new and huge
stroke of atrocity she plans within the house

to beat down the beloved beyond hope of healing?
Rescue is far away.

CHORUS

I can make nothing of these prophecies. The rest
I understood; the city is full of the sound of them.

CASSANDRA

So cruel then, that you can do this thing?
The husband of your own bed
to bathe bright with water—how shall I speak the end?
This thing shall be done with speed. The hand gropes
    now, and the other
hand follows in turn.

CHORUS

No, I am lost. After the darkness of her speech
I go bewildered in a mist of prophecies.

CASSANDRA

No, no, see there! What is that thing that shows?
Is it some net of death?
Or is the trap the woman there, the murderess?
Let now the slakeless fury in the race
rear up to howl aloud over this monstrous death.

CHORUS

Upon what demon in the house do you call, to raise
the cry of triumph? All your speech makes dark my
    hope.
And to the heart below trickles the pale drop
as in the hour of death

timed to our sunset and the mortal radiance.
Ruin is near, and swift.

CASSANDRA

See there, see there! Keep from his mate the bull.
Caught in the folded web's
entanglement she pinions him and with the black horn
strikes. And he crumples in the watered bath.
Guile, I tell you, and death there in the caldron
  wrought.

CHORUS

I am not proud in skill to guess at prophecies,
yet even I can see the evil in this thing.
From divination what good ever has come to men?
Art, and multiplication of words
drifting through tangled evil bring
terror to them that hear.

CASSANDRA

Alas, alas for the wretchedness of my ill-starred life.
This pain flooding the song of sorrow is mine alone.
Why have you brought me here in all unhappiness?
Why, why? Except to die with him? What else could
  be?

CHORUS

You are possessed of God, mazed at heart
to sing your own death
song, the wild lyric as
in clamor for Itys, Itys over and over again

her long life of tears weeping forever grieves
the brown nightingale.

CASSANDRA

Oh for the nightingale's pure song and a fate like hers.
With fashion of beating wings the gods clothed her
 about
and a sweet life gave her and without lamentation.
But mine is the sheer edge of the tearing iron.

CHORUS

Whence come, beat upon beat, driven of God,
vain passions of tears?
Whence your cries, terrified, clashing in horror,
in wrought melody and the singing speech?
Whence take you the marks to this path of prophecy
and speech of terror?

CASSANDRA

Oh marriage of Paris, death to the men beloved!
Alas, Scamandrus, water my fathers drank.
There was a time I too at your springs
drank and grew strong. Ah me,
for now beside the deadly rivers, Cocytus
and Acheron, I must cry out my prophecies.

CHORUS

What is this word, too clear, you have uttered now?
A child could understand.
And deep within goes the stroke of the dripping fang
as mortal pain at the trebled song of your agony
shivers the heart to hear.

CASSANDRA

O sorrow, sorrow of my city dragged to uttermost
  death.
O sacrifices my father made at the wall.
Flocks of the pastured sheep slaughtered there.
And no use at all
to save our city from its pain inflicted now.
And I too, with brain ablaze in fever, shall go down.

CHORUS

This follows the run of your song.
Is it, in cruel force of weight,
some divinity kneeling upon you brings
the death song of your passionate suffering?
I can not see the end.

CASSANDRA

No longer shall my prophecies like some young girl
new-married glance from under veils, but bright and
    strong
as winds blow into morning and the sun's uprise
shall wax along the swell like some great wave, to burst
at last upon the shining of this agony.
Now I will tell you plainly and from no cryptic speech;
bear me then witness, running at my heels upon
the scent of these old brutal things done long ago.
There is a choir that sings as one, that shall not again
leave this house ever; the song thereof breaks harsh
    with menace.
And drugged to double fury on the wine of men's
blood shed, there lurks forever here a drunken rout
of ingrown vengeful spirits never to be cast forth.

Hanging above the hall they chant their song of hate
and the old sin; and taking up the strain in turn
spit curses on that man who spoiled his brother's bed.
Did I go wide, or hit, like a real archer? Am I
some swindling seer who hawks his lies from door to
    door?
Upon your oath, bear witness that I know by heart
the legend of ancient wickedness within this house.

CHORUS

And how could an oath, though cast in rigid honesty,
do any good? And still we stand amazed at you,
reared in an alien city far beyond the sea,
how can you strike, as if you had been there, the truth.

CASSANDRA

Apollo was the seer who set me to this work.

CHORUS

Struck with some passion for you, and himself a god?

CASSANDRA

There was a time I blushed to speak about these things.

CHORUS

True; they who prosper take on airs of vanity.

CASSANDRA

Yes, then; he wrestled with me, and he breathed
    delight.

CHORUS

Did you come to the getting of children then, as people
    do?

CASSANDRA

I promised that to Loxias, but I broke my word.

CHORUS

Were you already ecstatic in the skills of God?

CASSANDRA

Yes; even then I read my city's destinies.

CHORUS

So Loxias' wrath did you no harm? How could that be?

CASSANDRA

For this my trespass, none believed me ever again.

CHORUS

But we do; all that you foretell seems true to us.

CASSANDRA

But this is evil, see!
Now once again the pain of grim, true prophecy
shivers my whirling brain in a storm of things foreseen.
Look there, see what is hovering above the house,
so small and young, imaged as in the shadow of dreams,
like children almost, killed by those most dear to them,
and their hands filled with their own flesh, as food to
    eat.
I see them holding out the inward parts, the vitals,
oh pitiful, that meat their father tasted of. . . .
I tell you: There is one that plots vengeance for this,
the strengthless lion rolling in his master's bed,
who keeps, ah me, the house against his lord's return;

my lord too, now that I wear the slave's yoke on my
   neck.
King of the ships, who tore up Ilium by the roots,
what does he know of this accursed bitch, who licks
his hand, who fawns on him with lifted ears, who like
a secret death shall strike the coward's stroke, nor fail?
No, this is daring when the female shall strike down
the male. What can I call her and be right? What beast
of loathing? Viper double-fanged, or Scylla witch
holed in the rocks and bane of men that range the sea;
smoldering mother of death to smoke relentless hate
on those most dear. How she stood up and howled
   aloud
and unashamed, as at the breaking point of battle,
in feigned gladness for his salvation from the sea!
What does it matter now if men believe or no?
What is to come will come. And soon you too will
   stand
beside, to murmur in pity that my words were true.

CHORUS

Thyestes' feast upon the flesh of his own children
I understand in terror at the thought, and fear
is on me hearing truth and no tale fabricated.
The rest: I heard it, but wander still far from the
   course.

CASSANDRA

I tell you, you shall look on Agamemnon dead.

CHORUS

Peace, peace, poor woman; put those bitter lips to sleep.

CASSANDRA

Useless; there is no god of healing in this story.

CHORUS

Not if it must be; may it somehow fail to come.

CASSANDRA

Prayers, yes; they do not pray; they plan to strike, and kill.

CHORUS

What man is it who moves this beastly thing to be?

CASSANDRA

What man? You did mistake my divination then.

CHORUS

It may be; I could not follow through the schemer's plan.

CASSANDRA

Yet I know Greek; I think I know it far too well.

CHORUS

And Pythian oracles are Greek, yet hard to read.

CASSANDRA

Oh, flame and pain that sweeps me once again! My lord,
Apollo, King of Light, the pain, aye me, the pain!
This is the woman-lioness, who goes to bed
with the wolf, when her proud lion ranges far away,
and she will cut me down; as a wife mixing drugs
she wills to shred the virtue of my punishment

into her bowl of wrath as she makes sharp the blade
against her man, death that he brought a mistress
    home.
Why do I wear these mockeries upon my body,
this staff of prophecy, these flowers at my throat?
At least I will spoil you before I die. Out, down,
break, damn you! This for all that you have done to me.
Make someone else, not me, luxurious in
    disaster. . . .
Lo now, this is Apollo who has stripped me here
of my prophetic robes. He watched me all the time
wearing this glory, mocked of all, my dearest ones
who hated me with all their hearts, so vain, so wrong;
called like some gypsy wandering from door to door
beggar, corrupt, half-starved, and I endured it all.
And now the seer has done with me, his prophetess,
and led me into such a place as this, to die.
Lost are my father's altars, but the block is there
to reek with sacrificial blood, my own. We two
must die, yet die not vengeless by the gods. For there
shall come one to avenge us also, born to slay
his mother, and to wreak death for his father's blood.
Outlaw and wanderer, driven far from his own land,
he will come back to cope these stones of inward hate.
For this is a strong oath and sworn by the high gods,
that he shall cast men headlong for his father felled.
Why am I then so pitiful? Why must I weep?
Since once I saw the citadel of Ilium
die as it died, and those who broke the city, doomed
by the gods, fare as they have fared accordingly,

I will go through with it. I too will take my fate.
I call as on the gates of death upon these gates
to pray only for this thing, that the stroke be true,
and that with no convulsion, with a rush of blood
in painless death, I may close up these eyes, and rest.

CHORUS

O woman much enduring and so greatly wise,
you have said much. But if this thing you know be true,
this death that comes upon you, how can you, serene,
walk to the altar like a driven ox of God?

CASSANDRA

Friends, there is no escape for any longer time.

CHORUS

Yet longest left in time is to be honored still.

CASSANDRA

The day is here and now; I can not win by flight.

CHORUS

Woman, be sure your heart is brave; you can take
much.

CASSANDRA

None but the unhappy people ever hear such praise.

CHORUS

Yet there is a grace on mortals who so nobly die.

CASSANDRA

Alas for you, father, and for your lordly sons.
Ah!

CHORUS

What now? What terror whirls you backward from the
door?

CASSANDRA

Foul, foul!

CHORUS

What foulness then, unless some horror in the mind?

CASSANDRA

That room within reeks with blood like a slaughter
house.

CHORUS

What then? Only these victims butchered at the hearth.

CASSANDRA

There is a breath about it like an open grave.

CHORUS

This is no Syrian pride of frankincense you mean.

CASSANDRA

So. I am going in, and mourning as I go
my death and Agamemnon's. Let my life be done.
Ah friends,
truly this is no wild bird fluttering at a bush,
nor vain my speech. Bear witness to me when I die,
when falls for me, a woman slain, another woman,
and when a man dies for this wickedly mated man.
Here in my death I claim this stranger's grace of you.

CHORUS

Poor wretch, I pity you the fate you see so clear.

CASSANDRA

Yet once more will I speak, and not this time my own
death's threnody. I call upon the Sun in prayer
against that ultimate shining when the avengers strike
these monsters down in blood, that they avenge as well
one simple slave who died, a small thing, lightly killed.

Alas, poor men, their destiny. When all goes well
a shadow will overthrow it. If it be unkind
one stroke of a wet sponge wipes all the picture out;
and that is far the most unhappy thing of all.

[Cassandra goes slowly into the house.]

CHORUS

High fortune is a thing slakeless
for mortals. There is no man who shall point
his finger to drive it back from the door
and speak the words: "Come no longer."
Now to this man the blessed ones have given
Priam's city to be captured
and return in the gods' honor.
Must he give blood for generations gone,
die for those slain and in death pile up
more death to come for the blood shed,
what mortal else who hears shall claim
he was born clear of the dark angel?

[Agamemnon, inside the house.]

Ah, I am struck a deadly blow and deep within!

CHORUS

Silence: who cried out that he was stabbed to death
within the house?

AGAMEMNON

Ah me, again, they struck again. I am wounded twice.

CHORUS

How the king cried out aloud to us! I believe the thing
is done.
Come, let us put our heads together, try to find some
safe way out.

[*The members of the Chorus go about
distractedly, each one speaking in turn.*]

Listen, let me tell you what I think is best to do.
Let the herald call all citizens to rally here.

No, better to burst in upon them now, at once,
and take them with the blood still running from their
blades.

I am with this man and I cast my vote to him.
Act now. This is the perilous and instant time.

Anyone can see it, by these first steps they have taken,
they purpose to be tyrants here upon our city.

Yes, for we waste time, while they trample to the
ground
deliberation's honor, and their hands sleep not.

I can not tell which counsel of yours to call my own.
It is the man of action who can plan as well.

I feel as he does; nor can I see how by words
we shall set the dead man back upon his feet again.

Do you mean, to drag our lives out long, that we must
    yield
to the house shamed, and leadership of such as these?

No, we can never endure that; better to be killed.
Death is a softer thing by far than tyranny.

Shall we, by no more proof than that he cried in pain,
be sure, as by divination, that our lord is dead?

Yes, we should know what is true before we break our
    rage.
Here is sheer guessing and far different from sure
    knowledge.

From all sides the voices multiply to make me choose
this course; to learn first how it stands with
    Agamemnon.

> [*The doors of the palace open, disclosing the
> bodies of Agamemnon and Cassandra, with
> Clytaemestra standing over them.*]

CLYTAEMESTRA
Much have I said before to serve necessity,

but I will take no shame now to unsay it all.
How else could I, arming hate against hateful men
disguised in seeming tenderness, fence high the nets
of ruin beyond overleaping? Thus to me
the conflict born of ancient bitterness is not
a thing new thought upon, but pondered deep in time.
I stand now where I struck him down. The thing is
    done.
Thus have I wrought, and I will not deny it now.
That he might not escape nor beat aside his death,
as fishermen cast their huge circling nets, I spread
deadly abundance of rich robes, and caught him fast.
I struck him twice. In two great cries of agony
he buckled at the knees and fell. When he was down
I struck him the third blow, in thanks and reverence
to Zeus the lord of dead men underneath the ground.
Thus he went down, and the life struggled out of him;
and as he died he spattered me with the dark red
and violent driven rain of bitter savored blood
to make me glad, as gardens stand among the showers
of God in glory at the birthtime of the buds.

These being the facts, elders of Argos assembled here,
be glad, if it be your pleasure; but for me, I glory.
Were it religion to pour wine above the slain,
this man deserved, more than deserved, such
    sacrament.
He filled our cup with evil things unspeakable
and now himself come home has drunk it to the dregs.

CHORUS

We stand here stunned. How can you speak this way, with mouth
so arrogant, to vaunt above your fallen lord?

CLYTAEMESTRA

You try me out as if I were a woman and vain;
but my heart is not fluttered as I speak before you.
You know it. You can praise or blame me as you wish;
it is all one to me. That man is Agamemnon,
my husband; he is dead; the work of this right hand
that struck in strength of righteousness. And that is
that.

CHORUS

Woman, what evil thing planted upon the earth
or dragged from the running salt sea could you have
tasted now
to wear such brutality and walk in the people's hate?
You have cast away, you have cut away. You shall go
homeless now,
crushed with men's bitterness.

CLYTAEMESTRA

Now it is I you doom to be cast out from my city
with men's hate heaped and curses roaring in my ears.
Yet look upon this dead man; you would not cross him
once
when with no thought more than as if a beast had died,
when his ranged pastures swarmed with the deep fleece
of flocks,

he slaughtered like a victim his own child, my pain
grown into love, to charm away the winds of Thrace.
Were you not bound to hunt him then clear of this soil
for the guilt stained upon him? Yet you hear what I
have done, and lo, you are a stern judge. But I say to
   you:
go on and threaten me, but know that I am ready,
if fairly you can beat me down beneath your hand,
for you to rule; but if the god grant otherwise,
you shall be taught—too late, for sure—to keep your
   place.

CHORUS

Great your design, your speech is a clamor of pride.
Swung to the red act drives the fury within your brain
signed clear in the splash of blood over your eyes.
Yet to come is stroke given for stroke
vengeless, forlorn of friends.

CLYTAEMESTRA

Now hear you this, the right behind my sacrament:
By my child's Justice driven to fulfilment, by
her Wrath and Fury, to whom I sacrificed this man,
the hope that walks my chambers is not traced with
   fear
while yet Aegisthus makes the fire shine on my hearth,
my good friend, now as always, who shall be for us
the shield of our defiance, no weak thing; while he,
this other, is fallen, stained with this woman you
   behold,

plaything of all the golden girls at Ilium;
and here lies she, the captive of his spear, who saw
wonders, who shared his bed, the wise in revelations
and loving mistress, who yet knew the feel as well
of the men's rowing benches. Their reward is not
unworthy. He lies there; and she who swanlike cried
aloud her lyric mortal lamentation out
is laid against his fond heart, and to me has given
a delicate excitement to my bed's delight.

CHORUS

O that in speed, without pain
and the slow bed of sickness
death could come to us now, death that forever
carries sleep without ending, now that our lord is down,
our shield, kindest of men,
who for a woman's grace suffered so much,
struck down at last by a woman.

Alas, Helen, wild heart
for the multitudes, for the thousand lives
you killed under Troy's shadow,
you alone, to shine in man's memory
as blood flower never to be washed out. Surely a demon
then
of death walked in the house, men's agony.

CLYTAEMESTRA

No, be not so heavy, nor yet draw down
in prayer death's ending,

neither turn all wrath against Helen
for men dead, that she alone killed
all those Danaan lives, to work
the grief that is past all healing.

CHORUS

Divinity that kneel on this house and the two
strains of the blood of Tantalus,
in the hands and hearts of women you steer
the strength tearing my heart.
Standing above the corpse, obscene
as some carrion crow she sings
the crippled song and is proud.

CLYTAEMESTRA

Thus have you set the speech of your lips
straight, calling by name
the spirit thrice glutted that lives in this race.
From him deep in the nerve is given
the love and the blood drunk, that before
the old wound dries, it bleeds again.

CHORUS

Surely it is a huge
and heavy spirit bending the house you cry;
alas, the bitter glory
of a doom that shall never be done with;
and all through Zeus, Zeus,
first cause, prime mover.
For what thing without Zeus is done among mortals?
What here is without God's blessing?

O king, my king
how shall I weep for you?
What can I say out of my heart of pity?
Caught in this spider's web you lie,
Your life gasped out in indecent death,
struck prone to this shameful bed
by your lady's hand of treachery
and the stroke twin edged of the iron.

CLYTAEMESTRA

Can you claim I have done this?
Speak of me never
more as the wife of Agamemnon.
In the shadow of this corpse's queen
the old stark avenger
of Atreus for his revel of hate
struck down this man,
last blood for the slaughtered children.

CHORUS

What man shall testify
your hands are clean of this murder?
How? How? Yet from his father's blood
might swarm some fiend to guide you.
The black ruin that shoulders
through the streaming blood of brothers
strides at last where he shall win requital
for the children who were eaten.

O king, my king
how shall I weep for you?

What can I say out of my heart of pity?
Caught in this spider's web you lie,
your life gasped out in indecent death,
struck prone to this shameful bed
by your lady's hand of treachery
and the stroke twin edged of the iron.

CLYTAEMESTRA

No shame, I think, in the death given
this man. And did he not
first of all in this house wreak death
by treachery?
The flower of this man's love and mine,
Iphigeneia of the tears
he dealt with even as he has suffered.
Let his speech in death's house be not loud.
With the sword he struck,
with the sword he paid for his own act.

CHORUS

My thoughts are swept away and I go bewildered.
Where shall I turn the brain's
activity in speed when the house is falling?
There is fear in the beat of the blood rain breaking
wall and tower. The drops come thicker.
Still fate grinds on yet more stones the blade
for more acts of terror.

Earth, my earth, why did you not fold me under
before ever I saw this man lie dead
fenced by the tub in silver?

Who shall bury him? Who shall mourn him?
Shall you dare this who have killed
your lord? Make lamentation,
render the graceless grace to his soul
for huge things done in wickedness?
Who over this great man's grave shall lay
the blessing of tears
worked soberly from a true heart?

CLYTAEMESTRA

Not for you to speak of such tendance.
Through us he fell,
by us he died; we shall bury.
There will be no tears in this house for him.
It must be Iphigeneia
his child, who else,
shall greet her father by the whirling stream
and the ferry of tears
to close him in her arms and kiss him.

CHORUS

Here is anger for anger. Between them
who shall judge lightly?
The spoiler is robbed; he killed, he has paid.
The truth stands ever beside God's throne
eternal: he who has wrought shall pay; that is law.
Then who shall tear the curse from their blood?
The seed is stiffened to ruin.

CLYTAEMESTRA

You see truth in the future

at last. Yet I wish
to seal my oath with the Spirit
in the house: I will endure all things as they stand
now, hard though it be. Hereafter
let him go forth to make bleed with death
and guilt the houses of others.
I will take some small
measure of our riches, and be content
that I swept from these halls
the murder, the sin, and the fury.

[*Aegisthus enters, followed at a little
distance by his armed bodyguard.*]

AEGISTHUS

O splendor and exaltation of this day of doom!
Now I can say once more that the high gods look down
on mortal crimes to vindicate the right at last,
now that I see this man—sweet sight—before me here
sprawled in the tangling nets of fury, to atone
the calculated evil of his father's hand.
For Atreus, this man's father, King of Argolis—
I tell you the clear story—drove my father forth,
Thyestes, his own brother, who had challenged him
in his king's right—forth from his city and his home.
Yet sad Thyestes came again to supplicate
the hearth, and win some grace, in that he was not
    slain
nor soiled the doorstone of his fathers with blood
    spilled.

Not his own blood. But Atreus, this man's godless sire,
angrily hospitable set a feast for him,
in seeming a glad day of fresh meat slain and good
cheer; then served my father his own children's flesh
to feed on. For he carved away the extremities,
hands, feet, and cut the flesh apart, and covered them
served in a dish to my father at his table apart,
who with no thought for the featureless meal before
    him ate
that ghastly food whose curse works now before your
    eyes.
But when he knew the terrible thing that he had done,
he spat the dead meat from him with a cry, and reeled
spurning the table back to heel with strength the curse:
"Thus crash in ruin all the seed of Pleisthenes."
Out of such acts you see this dead man stricken here,
and it was I, in my right, who wrought this murder, I
third born to my unhappy father, and with him
driven, a helpless baby in arms, to banishment.
Yet I grew up, and justice brought me home again,
till from afar I laid my hands upon this man,
since it was I who pieced together the fell plot.
Now I can die in honor again, if die I must,
having seen him caught in the cords of his just
    punishment.

CHORUS

Aegisthus, this strong vaunting in distress is vile.
You claim that you deliberately killed the king,

you, and you only, wrought the pity of this death.
I tell you then: There shall be no escape, your head
shall face the stones of anger from the people's hands.

AEGISTHUS

So loud from you, stooped to the meanest rowing bench
with the ship's masters lordly on the deck above?
You are old men; well, you shall learn how hard it is
at your age, to be taught how to behave yourselves.
But there are chains, there is starvation with its pain,
excellent teachers of good manners to old men,
wise surgeons and exemplars. Look! Can you not see it?
Lash not at the goads for fear you hit them, and be
    hurt.

CHORUS

So then you, like a woman, waited the war out
here in the house, shaming the master's bed with lust,
and planned against the lord of war this treacherous
    death?

AEGISTHUS

It is just such words as these will make you cry in pain.
Not yours the lips of Orpheus, no, quite otherwise,
whose voice of rapture dragged all creatures in his train.
You shall be dragged, for baby whimperings sobbed out
in rage. Once broken, you will be easier to deal with.

CHORUS

How shall you be lord of the men of Argos, you
who planned the murder of this man, yet could not dare
to act it out, and cut him down with your own hand?

AEGISTHUS

No, clearly the deception was the woman's part,
and I was suspect, that had hated him so long.
Still with his money I shall endeavor to control
the citizens. The mutinous man shall feel the yoke
drag at his neck, no cornfed racing colt that runs
free traced; but hunger, grim companion of the dark
dungeon shall see him broken to the hand at last.

CHORUS

But why, why then, you coward, could you not have
    slain
your man yourself? Why must it be his wife who killed,
to curse the country and the gods within the ground?
Oh, can Orestes live, be somewhere in sunlight still?
Shall fate grown gracious ever bring him back again
in strength of hand to overwhelm these murderers?

AEGISTHUS

You shall learn then, since you stick to stubbornness of
    mouth and hand.
Up now from your cover, my henchmen: here is work
    for you to do.

CHORUS

Look, they come! Let every man clap fist upon his
    hilted sword.

AEGISTHUS

I too am sword-handed against you; I am not afraid of
    death.

CHORUS

Death you said and death it shall be; we take up the
   word of fate.

CLYTAEMESTRA

No, my dearest, dearest of all men, we have done
   enough. No more
violence. Here is a monstrous harvest and a bitter
   reaping time.
There is pain enough already. Let us not be bloody now.
Honored gentlemen of Argos, go to your homes now
   and give way
to the stress of fate and season. We could not do
   otherwise
than we did. If this is the end of suffering, we can be
   content
broken as we are by the brute heel of angry destiny.
Thus a woman speaks among you. Shall men deign to
   understand?

AEGISTHUS

Yes, but think of these foolish lips that blossom into
   leering gibes,
think of the taunts they spit against me daring destiny
   and power,
sober opinion lost in insults hurled against my majesty.

CHORUS

It was never the Argive way to grovel at a vile man's
   feet.

AEGISTHUS

I shall not forget this; in the days to come I shall be
there.

CHORUS

Nevermore, if God's hand guiding brings Orestes home
again.

AEGISTHUS

Exiles feed on empty dreams of hope. I know it. I was
one.

CHORUS

Have your way, gorge and grow fat, soil justice, while
the power is yours.

AEGISTHUS

You shall pay, make no mistake, for this misguided
insolence.

CHORUS

Crow and strut, brave cockerel by your hen; you have
no threats to fear.

CLYTAEMESTRA

These are howls of impotent rage; forget them, dearest;
you and I
have the power; we two shall bring good order to our
house at least.

> [*They enter the house. The doors close. All
> persons leave the stage.*]

THE LIBATION
BEARERS

CHARACTERS

ORESTES, SON OF AGAMEMNON AND CLYTAEMESTRA

PYLADES, HIS FRIEND

ELECTRA, HIS SISTER

CHORUS, OF FOREIGN SERVING-WOMEN

A SERVANT (DOORKEEPER)

CLYTAEMESTRA, NOW WIFE OF AEGISTHUS,
QUEEN OF ARGOS

CILISSA, THE NURSE

AEGISTHUS, NOW KING OF ARGOS

A FOLLOWER OF AEGISTHUS

VARIOUS ATTENDANTS OF ORESTES, CLYTAEMESTRA,
AEGISTHUS (SILENT PARTS)

THE LIBATION BEARERS

SCENE: *Argos, at the tomb of Agamemnon.*

[Enter, as travelers, Orestes and Pylades.]

ORESTES

Hermes, lord of the dead, who watch over the powers
of my fathers, be my savior and stand by my claim.
Here is my own soil that I walk. I have come home;
and by this mounded gravebank I invoke my sire
to hear, to listen.
Here is a lock of hair for Inachus, who made
me grow to manhood. Here a strand to mark my grief.
I was not by, my father, to mourn for your death
nor stretched my hand out when they took your corpse
      away.

*[The chorus, with Electra, enter from
the side.]*

But what can this mean that I see, this group that
      comes
of women veiled in dignities of black? At what
sudden occurrence can I guess? Is this some new
wound struck into our house? I think they bring these
      urns
to pour, in my father's honor, to appease the powers
below. Can I be right? Surely, I think I see
Electra, my own sister, walk in bitter show

of mourning. Zeus, Zeus, grant me vengeance for my
father's
murder. Stand and fight beside me, of your grace.

Pylades, stand we out of their way. So may I learn
the meaning of these women; what their prayer would
ask.

CHORUS
I came in haste out of the house
to carry libations, hurt by the hard stroke of hands.
My cheek shows bright, ripped in the bloody furrows
of nails gashing the skin.
This is my life: to feed the heart on hard-drawn breath.
And in my grief, with splitting weft
of ragtorn linen across my heart's
brave show of robes
came sound of my hands' strokes
in sorrows whence smiles are fled.

Terror, the dream diviner of
this house, belled clear, shuddered the skin, blew wrath
from sleep, a cry in night's obscure watches,
a voice of fear deep in the house,
dropping deadweight in women's inner chambers.
And they who read the dream meanings
and spoke under guarantee of God
told how under earth
dead men held a grudge still
and smoldered at their murderers.

On such grace without grace, evil's turning aside
(Earth, Earth, kind mother!)
bent, the godless woman
sends me forth. But terror
is on me for this word let fall.
What can wash off the blood once spilled upon the
    ground?
O hearth soaked in sorrow,
o wreckage of a fallen house.
Sunless and where men fear to walk
the mists huddle upon this house
where the high lords have perished.

The pride not to be warred with, fought with, not to be
    beaten down
of old, sounded in all men's
ears, in all hearts sounded,
has shrunk away. A man
goes in fear. High fortune,
this in man's eyes is god and more than god is this.
But, as a beam balances, so
sudden disasters wait, to strike
some in the brightness, some in gloom
of half dark in their elder time.
Desperate night holds others.

Through too much glut of blood drunk by our fostering
    ground
the vengeful gore is caked and hard, will not drain
    through.

The deep-run ruin carries away
the man of guilt. Swarming infection boils within.

For one who handles the bridal close, there is no cure.
All the world's waters running in a single drift
may try to wash blood from the hand
of the stained man; they only bring new blood guilt on.

But as for me: gods have forced on my city
resisted fate. From our fathers' houses
they led us here, to take the lot of slaves.
And mine it is to wrench my will, and consent
to their commands, right or wrong,
to beat down my edged hate.
And yet under veils I weep
the vanities that have killed
my lord; and freeze with sorrow in the secret heart.

ELECTRA

Attendant women, who order our house, since you
are with me in this supplication and escort
me here, be also my advisers in this rite.
What shall I say, as I pour out these outpourings
of sorrow? How say the good word, how make my
     prayer
to my father? Shall I say I bring it to the man
beloved, from a loving wife, and mean my mother? I
have not the daring to say this, nor know what else
to say, as I pour this liquid on my father's tomb.
Shall I say this sentence, regular in human use:

"Grant good return to those who send to you these
    flowers
of honor: gifts to match the . . . evil they have done."

Or, quiet and dishonored, as my father died
shall I pour out this offering for the ground to drink,
and go, like one who empties garbage out of doors,
and turn my eyes, and throw the vessel far away.

Dear friends, in this deliberation stay with me.
We hold a common hatred in this house. Do not
for fear of any, hide your thought inside your heart.
The day of destiny waits for the free man as well
as for the man enslaved beneath an alien hand.
If you know any better course than mine, tell me.

CHORUS

In reverence for your father's tomb as if it were
an altar, I will speak my heart's thought, as you ask.

ELECTRA

Tell me then, please, as you respect my father's grave.

CHORUS

Say words of grace for those of good will, as you pour.

ELECTRA

Whom of those closest to me can I call my friend?

CHORUS

Yourself first; all who hate Aegisthus after that.

ELECTRA

You mean these prayers shall be for you, and for
myself?

CHORUS

You see it now; but it is you whose thought this is.

ELECTRA

Is there some other we should bring in on our side?

CHORUS

Remember Orestes, though he wanders far away.

ELECTRA

That was well spoken; you did well reminding me.

CHORUS

Remember, too, the murderers, and against them . . .

ELECTRA

What shall I say? Guide and instruct my ignorance.

CHORUS

Invoke the coming of some man, or more than man.

ELECTRA

To come to judge them, or to give them punishment?

CHORUS

Say simply: "one to kill them, for the life they took."

ELECTRA

I can ask this, and not be wrong in the gods' eyes?

CHORUS

May you not hurt your enemy, when he struck first?

ELECTRA

Almighty herald of the world above, the world
below: Hermes, lord of the dead, help me; announce
my prayers to the charmed spirits underground, who
   watch
over my father's house, that they may hear. Tell Earth
herself, who brings all things to birth, who gives them
   strength,
then gathers their big yield into herself at last.
I myself pour these lustral waters to the dead,
and speak, and call upon my father: Pity me;
pity your own Orestes. How shall we be lords
in our house? We have been sold, and go as wanderers
because our mother bought herself, for us, a man,
Aegisthus, he who helped her hand to cut you down.
Now I am what a slave is, and Orestes lives
outcast from his great properties, while they go proud
in the high style and luxury of what you worked
to win. By some good fortune let Orestes come
back home. Such is my prayer, my father. Hear me;
   hear.
And for myself, grant that I be more temperate
of heart than my mother; that I act with purer hand.

Such are my prayers for us; but for our enemies,
father, I pray that your avenger come, that they
who killed you shall be killed in turn, as they deserve.
Between my prayer for good and prayer for good I set
this prayer for evil; and I speak it against Them.
For us, bring blessings up into the world. Let Earth
and conquering Justice, and all gods beside, give aid.

Such are my prayers; and over them I pour these drink
offerings. Yours the strain now, yours to make them
   flower
with mourning song, and incantation for the dead.

CHORUS

Let the tear fall, that clashes as it dies
as died our fallen lord;
die on this mound that fences good from evil,
washing away the death stain accursed
of drink offerings shed. Hear me, oh hear, my lord,
majesty hear me from your dark heart; oh hear.
Let one come, in strength
of spear, some man at arms who will set free the house
holding the Scythian bow backbent in his hands,
a barbarous god of war spattering arrows
or closing to slash, with sword hilted fast to his hand.

ELECTRA

Father, the earth has drunk my offerings poured to you.
Something has happened here, my women. Help me
   now.

CHORUS

Speak, if you will. My heart is in a dance of fear.

ELECTRA

Someone has cut a strand of hair and laid it on
the tomb.

CHORUS

          What man? Or was it some deep-waisted girl?

ELECTRA

There is a mark, which makes it plain for any to guess.

CHORUS

Explain, and let your youth instruct my elder age.

ELECTRA

No one could have cut off this strand, except myself.

CHORUS

Those others, whom it would have become, are full of hate.

ELECTRA

Yet here it is, and for appearance matches well . . .

CHORUS

With whose hair? Tell me. This is what I long to know. . . .

ELECTRA

With my own hair. It is almost exactly like.

CHORUS

Can it then be a secret gift from Orestes?

ELECTRA

It seems that it must be nobody's hair but his.

CHORUS

Did Orestes dare to come back here? How could this be?

ELECTRA

He sent this severed strand, to do my father grace.

CHORUS

It will not stop my tears if you are right. You mean
that he can never again set foot upon this land.

ELECTRA

The bitter wash has surged upon my heart as well.
I am struck through, as by the cross-stab of a sword,
and from my eyes the thirsty and unguarded drops
burst in a storm of tears like winter rain, as I
look on this strand of hair. How could I think some
    other
man, some burgess, could ever go grand in hair like
    this?
She never could have cut it, she who murdered him
and is my mother, but no mother in her heart
which has assumed God's hate and hates her children.
    No.
And yet, how can I say in open outright confidence
this is a treasured token from the best beloved
of men to me, Orestes? Does hope fawn on me?
Ah
I wish it had the kind voice of a messenger
so that my mind would not be torn in two, I not
shaken, but it could tell me plain to throw this strand
away as vile, if it was cut from a hated head,
or like a brother could have mourned with me, and
    been
a treasured splendor for my father, and his grave.

The gods know, and we call upon the gods; they know
how we are spun in circles like seafarers, in

what storms. But if we are to win, and our ship live,
from one small seed could burgeon an enormous tree.

But see, here is another sign. Footprints are here.
The feet that made them are alike, and look like mine.
There are two sets of footprints: of the man who gave
his hair, and one who shared the road with him. I step
where he has stepped, and heelmarks, and the space
    between
his heel and toe are like the prints I make. Oh, this
is torment, and my wits are going.

> [*Orestes comes from his place of*
> *concealment.*]

ORESTES

Pray for what is to come, and tell the gods that they
have brought your former prayers to pass. Pray for
success.

ELECTRA

Upon what ground? What have I won yet from the
gods?

ORESTES

You have come in sight of all you long since prayed to
see.

ELECTRA

How did you know what man was subject of my
prayer?

ORESTES

I know about Orestes, how he stirred your heart.

ELECTRA

Yes; but how am I given an answer to my prayers?

ORESTES

Look at me. Look for no one closer to you than I.

ELECTRA

Is this some net of treachery, friend, you catch me in?

ORESTES

Then I must be contriving plots against myself.

ELECTRA

It is your pleasure to laugh at my unhappiness.

ORESTES

I only mock my own then, if I laugh at you.

ELECTRA

Are you really Orestes? Can I call you by that name?

ORESTES

You see my actual self and are slow to learn. And yet
you saw this strand of hair I cut in sign of grief
and shuddered with excitement, for you thought you
    saw
me, and again when you were measuring my tracks.
Now lay the severed strand against where it was cut
and see how well your brother's hair matches my head.
Look at this piece of weaving, the work of your hand
with its blade strokes and figured design of beasts. No,
    no,
control yourself, and do not lose your head for joy.
I know those nearest to us hate us bitterly.

ELECTRA

O dearest, treasured darling of my father's house,
hope of the seed of our salvation, wept for, trust
your strength of hand, and win your father's house
   again.
O bright beloved presence, you bring back four lives
to me. To call you father is constraint of fact,
and all the love I could have borne my mother turns
your way, while she is loathed as she deserves; my love
for a pitilessly slaughtered sister turns to you.
And now you were my steadfast brother after all.
You alone bring me honor; but let Force, and Right,
and Zeus almighty, third with them, be on your side.

ORESTES

Zeus, Zeus, direct all that we try to do. Behold
the orphaned children of the eagle-father, now
that he has died entangled in the binding coils
of the deadly viper, and the young he left behind
are worn with hunger of starvation, not full grown
to bring their shelter slain food, as their father did.
I, with my sister, whom I name, Electra here,
stand in your sight, children whose father is lost. We
   both
are driven from the house that should be ours. If you
destroy these fledgelings of a father who gave you
sacrifice and high honor, from what hand like his
shall you be given the sacred feast which is your right?
Destroy the eagle's brood, and you have no more means
to send your signs to mortals for their strong belief;
nor, if the stump rot through on this baronial tree,

shall it sustain your altars on sacrificial days.
Safe keep it: from a little thing you can raise up
a house to grandeur, though it now seem overthrown.

CHORUS

O children, silence! Saviors of your father's house,
be silent, children. Otherwise someone may hear
and for mere love of gossip carry news of all
you do, to those in power, to those I long to see
some day as corpses in the leaking pitch and flame.

ORESTES

The big strength of Apollo's oracle will not
forsake me. For he charged me to win through this
    hazard,
with divination of much, and speech articulate,
the winters of disaster under the warm heart
were I to fail against my father's murderers;
told me to cut them down in their own fashion, turn
to the bull's fury in the loss of my estates.
He said that else I must myself pay penalty
with my own life, and suffer much sad punishment;
spoke of the angers that come out of the ground from
    those
beneath who turn against men; spoke of sicknesses,
ulcers that ride upon the flesh, and cling, and with
wild teeth eat away the natural tissue, how on this
disease shall grow in turn a leprous fur. He spoke
of other ways again by which the avengers might
attack, brought to fulfilment from my father's blood.
For the dark arrow of the dead men underground

from those within my blood who fell and turn to call
upon me; madness and empty terror in the night
on one who sees clear and whose eyes move in the
  dark,
must tear him loose and shake him until, with all his
  bulk
degraded by the bronze-loaded lash, he lose his city.
And such as he can have no share in the communal
  bowl
allowed them, no cup filled for friends to drink. The
  wrath
of the father comes unseen on them to drive them back
from altars. None can take them in nor shelter them.
Dishonored and unloved by all the man must die
at last, shrunken and wasted away in painful death.

Shall I not trust such oracles as this? Or if
I do not trust them, here is work that must be done.
Here numerous desires converge to drive me on:
the god's urgency and my father's passion, and
with these the loss of my estates wears hard on me;
the thought that these my citizens, most high
  renowned
of men, who toppled Troy in show of courage, must
go subject to this brace of women; since his heart
is female; or, if it be not, that soon will show.

CHORUS

Almighty Destinies, by the will
of Zeus let these things

be done, in the turning of Justice.
For the word of hatred spoken, let hate
be a word fulfilled. The spirit of Right
cries out aloud and extracts atonement
due: blood stroke for the stroke of blood
shall be paid. Who acts, shall endure. So speaks
the voice of the age-old wisdom.

ORESTES

Father, o my dread father, what thing
can I say, can I accomplish
from this far place where I stand, to mark
and reach you there in your chamber
with light that will match your dark?
Yet it is called an action
of grace to mourn in style for the house,
once great, of the sons of Atreus.

CHORUS

Child, when the fire burns
and tears with teeth at the dead man
it can not wear out the heart of will.
He shows his wrath in the after
days. One dies, and is dirged.
Light falls on the man who killed him.
He is hunted down by the deathsong
for sires slain and for fathers,
disturbed, and stern, and enormous.

ELECTRA

Hear me, my father; hear in turn
all the tears of my sorrows.

Two children stand at your tomb to sing
the burden of your death chant.
Your grave is shelter to suppliants,
shelter to the outdriven.
What here is good; what escape from grief?
Can we outwrestle disaster?

CHORUS

Yet from such as this the god, if he will,
can work out strains that are fairer.
For dirges chanted over the grave
the winner's song in the lordly house;
bring home to new arms the beloved.

ORESTES

If only at Ilium,
father, and by some Lycian's hands
you had gone down at the spear's stroke,
you would have left high fame in your house,
in the going forth of your children
eyes' admiration;
founded the deep piled bank of earth
for grave by the doubled water
with light lift for your household;

CHORUS

loved then by those he loved
down there beneath the ground
who died as heroes, he would have held
state, and a lord's majesty,
vassal only to those most great,
the Kings of the under darkness.

For he was King on earth when he lived
over those whose hands held power of life
and death, and the staff of authority.

ELECTRA

No, but not under Troy's
ramparts, father, should you have died,
nor, with the rest of the spearstruck hordes
have found your grave by Scamandrus' crossing.
Sooner, his murderers
should have been killed, as he was,
by those they loved, and have found their death,
and men remote from this outrage
had heard the distant story.

CHORUS

Child, child, you are dreaming, since dreaming is a light
pastime, of fortune more golden than gold
or the Blessed Ones north of the North Wind.
But the stroke of the twofold lash is pounding
close, and powers gather under ground
to give aid. The hands of those who are lords
are unclean, and these are accursed.
Power grows on the side of the children.

ORESTES

This cry has come to your ear
like a deep driven arrow.
Zeus, Zeus, force up from below
ground the delayed destruction

on the hard heart and the daring
hand, for the right of our fathers.

CHORUS

May I claim right to close the deathsong
chanted in glory across
the man speared and the woman
dying. Why darken what deep within me forever
flitters? Long since against the heart's
stem a bitter wind has blown
thin anger and burdened hatred.

ELECTRA

May Zeus, from all shoulder's strength,
pound down his fist upon them,
ohay, smash their heads.
Let the land once more believe.
There has been wrong done. I ask for right.
Hear me, Earth. Hear me, grandeurs of Darkness.

CHORUS

It is but law that when the red drops have been spilled
upon the ground they cry aloud for fresh
blood. For the death act calls out on Fury
to bring out of those who were slain before
new ruin on ruin accomplished.

ORESTES

Hear me, you lordships of the world below.
Behold in assembled power, curses come from the dead,
behold the last of the sons of Atreus, foundering

lost, without future, cast
from house and right. O god, where shall we turn?

CHORUS

The heart jumped in me once again
to hear this unhappy prayer.
I was disconsolate then
and the deep heart within
darkened to hear you speak it.
But when strength came back hope lifted
me again, and the sorrow
was gone and the light was on me.

ELECTRA

Of what thing can we speak, and strike more close,
than of the sorrows they who bore us have given?
So let her fawn if she likes. It softens not.
For we are bloody like the wolf
and savage born from the savage mother.

CHORUS

I struck my breast in the stroke-style of the Arian,
the Cissian mourning woman,
and the hail-beat of the drifting fists was there to see
as the rising pace went in a pattern of blows
downward and upward until the crashing strokes
played on my hammered, my all-stricken head.

ELECTRA

O cruel, cruel
all daring mother, in cruel processional
with all his citizens gone,

with all sorrow for him forgotten
you dared bury your unbewept lord.

ORESTES

O all unworthy of him, that you tell me.
Shall she not pay for this dishonor
for all the immortals,
for all my own hands can do?
Let me but take her life and die for it.

CHORUS

Know then, they hobbled him beneath the armpits,
with his own hands. She wrought so, in his burial
to make his death a burden
beyond your strength to carry.
The mutilation of your father. Hear it.

ELECTRA

You tell of how my father was murdered. Meanwhile I
stood apart, dishonored, nothing worth,
in the dark corner, as you would kennel a vicious dog,
and burst in an outrush of tears, that came that day
where smiles would not, and hid the streaming of my
    grief.
Hear such, and carve the letters of it on your heart.

CHORUS

Let words such as these
drip deep in your ears, but on a quiet heart.
So far all stands as it stands;
what is to come, yourself burn to know.
You must be hard, give no ground, to win home.

ORESTES

I speak to you. Be with those you love, my father.

ELECTRA

And I, all in my tears, ask with him.

CHORUS

We gather into murmurous revolt. Hear
us, hear. Come back into the light.
Be with us against those we hate.

ORESTES

Warstrength shall collide with warstrength; right with
right.

ELECTRA

O gods, be just in what you bring to pass.

CHORUS

My flesh crawls as I listen to them pray.
The day of doom has waited long.
They call for it. It may come.

O pain grown into the race
and blood-dripping stroke
and grinding cry of disaster,
moaning and impossible weight to bear.
Sickness that fights all remedy.

Here in the house there lies
the cure for this, not to be brought
from outside, never from others

but in themselves, through the fierce wreck and
 bloodshed.
Here is a song sung to the gods beneath us.
Hear then, you blessed ones under the ground,
and answer these prayers with strength on our side,
free gift for your children's conquest.

ORESTES

Father, o King who died no kingly death, I ask
the gift of lordship at your hands, to rule your house.

ELECTRA

I too, my father, ask of you such grace as this:
to murder Aegisthus with strong hand, and then go free.

ORESTES

So shall your memory have the feasts that men honor
in custom. Otherwise when feasts are gay, and portions
burn for the earth, you shall be there, and none give
 heed.

ELECTRA

I too out of my own full dowership shall bring
libations for my bridal from my father's house.
Of all tombs, yours shall be the lordliest in my eyes.

ORESTES

O Earth, let my father emerge to watch me fight.

ELECTRA

Persephone, grant still the wonder of success.

ORESTES

Think of that bath, father, where you were stripped of
 life.

ELECTRA

Think of the casting net that they contrived for you.

ORESTES

They caught you like a beast in toils no bronzesmith
made.

ELECTRA

Rather, hid you in shrouds that were thought out in
shame.

ORESTES

Will you not waken, father, to these challenges?

ELECTRA

Will you not rear upright that best beloved head?

ORESTES

Send out your right to battle on the side of those
you love, or give us holds like those they caught you in.
For they threw you. Would you not see them thrown in
turn?

ELECTRA

Hear one more cry, father, from me. It is my last.
Your nestlings huddle suppliant at your tomb: look
forth
and pity them, female with the male strain alike.
Do not wipe out this seed of the Pelopidae.
So, though you died, you shall not yet be dead, for
when
a man dies, children are the voice of his salvation
afterward. Like corks upon the net, these hold

the drenched and flaxen meshes, and they will not
drown.
Hear us, then. Our complaints are for your sake, and if
you honor this our argument, you save yourself.

CHORUS

None can find fault with the length of this discourse
you drew
out, to show honor to a grave and fate unwept
before. The rest is action. Since your heart is set
that way, now you must strike and prove your destiny.

ORESTES

So. But I am not wandering from my strict course
when I ask why she sent these libations, for what cause
she acknowledges, too late, a crime for which there is
no cure. Here was a wretched grace brought to a man
dead and unfeeling. This I fail to understand.
The offerings are too small for the act done. Pour out
all your possessions to atone one act of blood,
you waste your work, it is all useless, reason says.
Explain me this, for I would learn it, if you know.

CHORUS

I know, child, I was there. It was the dreams she had.
The godless woman had been shaken in the night
by floating terrors, when she sent these offerings.

ORESTES

Do you know the dream, too? Can you tell it to me
right?

CHORUS

She told me herself. She dreamed she gave birth to a
snake.

ORESTES

What is the end of the story then? What is the point?

CHORUS

She laid it swathed for sleep as if it were a child.

ORESTES

A little monster. Did it want some kind of food?

CHORUS

She herself, in the dream, gave it her breast to suck.

ORESTES

How was her nipple not torn by such a beastly thing?

CHORUS

It was. The creature drew in blood along with the milk.

ORESTES

No void dream this. It is the vision of a man.

CHORUS

She woke screaming out of her sleep, shaky with fear,
as torches kindled all about the house, out of
the blind dark that had been on them, to comfort the
queen.
So now she sends these mourning offerings to be poured
and hopes they are medicinal for her disease.

ORESTES

But I pray to the earth and to my father's grave
that this dream is for me and that I will succeed.

See, I divine it, and it coheres all in one piece.
If this snake came out of the same place whence I
    came,
if she wrapped it in robes, as she wrapped me, and if
its jaws gaped wide around the breast that suckled me,
and if it stained the intimate milk with an outburst
of blood, so that for fright and pain she cried aloud,
it follows then, that as she nursed this hideous thing
of prophecy, she must be cruelly murdered. I
turn snake to kill her. This is what the dream portends.

CHORUS

I choose you my interpreter to read these dreams.
So may it happen. Now you must rehearse your side
in their parts. For some, this means the parts they must
    not play.

ORESTES

Simple to tell them. My sister here must go inside.
I charge her to keep secret what we have agreed,
so that, as they by treachery killed a man of high
degree, by treachery tangled in the self same net
they too shall die, in the way Loxias has ordained,
my lord Apollo, whose word was never false before.
Disguised as an outlander, for which I have all gear,
I shall go to the outer gates with Pylades
whom you see here. He is hereditary friend
and companion-in-arms of my house. We two shall both
    assume
the Parnassian dialect and imitate the way
they talk in Phocis. If none at the door will take us in
kindly, because the house is in a curse of ills,

we shall stay there, till anybody who goes by
the house will wonder why we are shut out, and say:
"why does Aegisthus keep the suppliant turned away
from his gates, if he is hereabouts and knows of this?"
But if I once cross the doorstone of the outer gates
and find my man seated upon my father's throne,
or if he comes down to confront me, and uplifts
his eyes to mine, then lets them drop again, be sure,
before he can say: "where does the stranger come
    from?" I
shall plunge my sword with lightning speed, and drop
    him dead.
Our Fury who is never starved for blood shall drink
for the third time a cupful of unwatered blood.

Electra, keep a careful eye on all within
the house, so that our plans will hold together. You,
women: I charge you, hold your tongues religiously.
Be silent if you must, or speak in the way that will
help us. And now I call upon the god who stands
close, to look on, and guide the actions of my sword.

> [*Exeunt Orestes and Pylades. Exit separately,*
> *Electra.*]

CHORUS

Numberless, the earth breeds
dangers, and the sober thought of fear.
The bending sea's arms swarm
with bitter, savage beasts.
Torches blossom to burn along

the high space between ground and sky.
Things fly, and things walk the earth.
Remember too
the storm and wrath of the whirlwind.

But who can recount all
the high daring in the will
of man, and in the stubborn hearts of women
the all-adventurous passions
that couple with man's overthrow.
The female force, the desperate
love crams its resisted way
on marriage and the dark embrace
of brute beasts, of mortal men.

Let him, who goes not on flimsy wings
of thought, learn from her,
Althaea, Thestius'
daughter: who maimed her child, and hard
of heart, in deliberate guile
set fire to the bloody torch, her own son's
agemate, that from the day he emerged
from the mother's womb crying
shared the measure of all his life
down to the marked death day.

And in the legends there is one more, a girl
of blood, figure of hate
who, for the enemy's
sake killed one near in blood, seduced by the wrought

golden necklace from Crete,
wherewith Minos bribed her. She sundered
from Nisus his immortal hair
as he all unsuspecting
breathed in a tranquil sleep. Foul wretch,
Hermes of death has got her now.

Since I recall cruelties from quarrels long
ago, in vain, and married love turned to bitterness
a house would fend far away
by curse; the guile, treacheries of the woman's heart
against a lord armored in
power, a lord his enemies revered,
I prize the hearth not inflamed within the house,
the woman's right pushed not into daring.

Of all foul things legends tell the Lemnian
outranks, a vile wizard's charm, detestable
so that man names a hideous
crime "Lemnian" in memory of their wickedness.
When once the gods loathe a breed
of men they go outcast and forgotten.
No man respects what the gods have turned against.
What of these tales I gather has no meaning?

The sword edges near the lungs.
It stabs deep, bittersharp,
and right drives it. For that which had no right
lies not yet stamped into the ground, although
one in sin transgressed Zeus' majesty.

Right's anvil stands staunch on the ground
and the smith, Destiny, hammers out the sword.
Delayed in glory, pensive from
the murk, Vengeance brings home at last
a child, to wipe out the stain of blood shed long ago.

[*The scene is now before the door of
Clytaemestra's palace, with the tomb of
Agamemnon well down stage. Enter Orestes
and Pylades.*]

ORESTES

In there! Inside! Does anyone hear me knocking at
the gate? I will try again. Is anyone at home?
Try a third time. I ask for someone to come from the
house,
if Aegisthus lets it welcome friendly visitors.

SERVANT [*inside*]

All right, I hear you. Where does the stranger come
from, then?

ORESTES

Announce me to the masters of the house. It is
to them I come, and I have news for them to hear.
And be quick, for the darkening chariot of night
leans to its course; the hour for wayfarers to drop
anchor in some place that entertains all travelers.
Have someone of authority in the house come out,
the lady of the place or, more appropriately,
its lord, for then no delicacy in speaking blurs

the spoken word. A man takes courage and speaks out
to another man, and makes clear everything he means.

[Enter Clytaemestra.]

CLYTAEMESTRA

Friends, tell me only what you would have, and it is
yours.
We have all comforts that go with a house like ours,
hot baths, and beds to charm away your weariness
with rest, and the regard of temperate eyes. But if
you have some higher business, more a matter of state,
that is the men's concern, and I will tell them of it.

ORESTES

I am a Daulian stranger out of Phocis. As
I traveled with my pack and my own following
making for Argos, where my feet are rested now,
I met a man I did not know, nor did he know
me, but he asked what way I took, and told me his.
It was a Phocian, Strophius; for he told me his name
and said: "Friend, since in any case you make for Argos,
remember carefully to tell Orestes' parents
that he is dead; please do not let it slip your mind.
Then, if his people decide to have him brought back
   home,
or bury him where he went to live, all outlander
forever, carry their requests again to me.
For as it is the bronze walls of an urn close in
the ashes of a man who has been deeply mourned."

So much I know, no more. But whether I now talk
with those who have authority and concern in this
I do not know. I think his father should be told.

CLYTAEMESTRA

Ah me. You tell us how we are stormed from head to
   heel.
Oh curse upon our house, bitter antagonist,
how far your eyes range. What was clean out of your
   way
your archery brings down with a distant deadly shot
to strip unhappy me of all I ever loved.
Even Orestes now! He was so well advised
to keep his foot clear of this swamp of death. But now
set down as traitor the hope that was our healer once
and made us look for a bright revel in our house.

ORESTES

I could have wished, with hosts so prosperous as you,
to have made myself known by some more gracious
   news
and so been entertained by you. For what is there
more kindly than the feeling between host and guest?
Yet it had been abuse of duty in my heart
had I not given so great a matter to his friends,
being so bound by promise and the stranger's rights.

CLYTAEMESTRA

You shall not find that your reception falls below
your worth, nor be any the less our friend for this.

Some other would have brought the news in any case.
But it is the hour for travelers who all day have trudged
the long road, to be given the rest that they deserve.
Escort this gentleman with his companion and
his men, to where our masculine friends are made at
    home.
Look after them, in manner worthy of a house
like ours; you are responsible for their good care.
Meanwhile, we shall communicate these matters to
the masters of the house, and with our numerous
    friends
deliberate the issues of this fatal news.

[Exeunt all but the Chorus.]

CHORUS

Handmaidens of this house, who help our cause,
how can our lips frame
some force that will show for Orestes?
O Lady Earth, Earth Queen, who now
ride mounded over the lord of ships
where the King's corpse lies buried,
hear us, help us.
Now the time breaks for Persuasion in stealth
to go down to the pit, with Hermes of death
and the dark, to direct
trial by the sword's fierce edge.
I think our newcomer is at his deadly work;
I see Orestes' old nurse coming forth, in tears.

[Enter Cilissa.]

Now where away, Cilissa, through the castle gates,
with sorrow as your hireless fellow-wayfarer?

CILISSA

The woman who is our mistress told me to make haste
and summon Aegisthus for the strangers, "so that he
can come and hear, as man to man, in more detail
this news that they have brought." She put a sad face
    on
before the servants, to hide the smile inside her eyes
over this work that has been done so happily
for her—though on this house the curse is now
    complete
from the plain story that the stranger men have
    brought.
But as for that Aegisthus, oh, he will be pleased
enough to hear the story. Poor unhappy me,
all my long-standing mixture of misfortunes, hard
burden enough, here in this house of Atreus,
when it befell me made the heart ache in my breast.
But never yet did I have to bear a hurt like this.
I took the other troubles bravely as they came:
but now, darling Orestes! I wore out my life
for him. I took him from his mother, brought him up.
There were times when he screamed at night and woke
    me from
my rest; I had to do many hard tasks, and now
useless; a baby is like a beast, it does not think
but you have to nurse it, do you not, the way it wants.
For the child still in swaddling clothes can not tell us

if he is hungry or thirsty, if he needs to make
water. Children's young insides are a law to
   themselves.
I needed second sight for this, and many a time
I think I missed, and had to wash the baby's clothes.
The nurse and laundrywoman had a combined duty
and that was I. I was skilled in both handicrafts,
and so Orestes' father gave him to my charge.
And now, unhappy, I am told that he is dead
and go to take the story to that man who has
defiled our house; he will be glad to hear such news.

CHORUS

Did she say he should come back armed in any way?

CILISSA

How, armed? Say it again. I do not understand.

CHORUS

Was he to come with bodyguards, or by himself?

CILISSA

She said to bring his followers, the men-at-arms.

CHORUS

Now, if you hate our master, do not tell him that,
but simply bid him come as quickly as he can
and cheerfully. In that way he will not take fright.
It is the messenger who makes the bent word straight.

CILISSA

But are you happy over what I have told you?

CHORUS

Perhaps: if Zeus might turn our evil wind to good.

CILISSA

How so? Orestes, once hope of the house, is gone.

CHORUS

Not yet. It would be a poor seer who saw it thus.

CILISSA

What is this? Have you some news that has not been told?

CHORUS

Go on and take your message, do as you were bid.
The gods' concerns are what concern only the gods.

CILISSA

I will go then and do all this as you have told
me to. May all be for the best. So grant us god.

[*Exit Cilissa.*]

CHORUS

Now to my supplication, Zeus,
father of Olympian gods,
grant that those who struggle hard to see
temperate things done in the house win their aim
in full. All that I spoke
was spoken in right. Yours, Zeus, to protect.

Zeus, Zeus, make him who is now
in the house stand above those who

hate. If you rear him to greatness,
double and three times
and blithely he will repay you.

See the colt of this man whom you loved
harnessed to the chariot
of suffering. Set upon the race he runs
sure control. Make us not see him break
stride, but clean down the course
hold the strain of his striding speed.

You that, deep in the house
sway their secret pride of wealth,
hear us, gods of sympathy.
For things done in time past
wash out the blood in fair-spoken verdict.
Let the old murder in
the house breed no more.

And you, who keep, magnificent, the hallowed and
    huge
cavern, o grant that the man's house lift up its head
and look on the shining of daylight
and liberty with eyes made
glad with gazing out from the helm of darkness.

And with right may the son
of Maia lend his hand, strong to send
wind fair for action, if he will.
Much else lies secret he may show at need.

He speaks the markless word, by
night hoods darkness on the eyes
nor shows more plainly when the day is there.

Then at last we shall sing
for deliverance of the house
the woman's song that sets the wind
fair, no thin drawn and grief
struck wail, but this: "The ship sails fair."
My way, mine, the advantage piles here, with wreck
and ruin far from those I love.

Be not fear struck when your turn comes in the action
but with a great cry *Father*
when she cries *Child* to you
go on through with the innocent murder.

Yours to raise high within
your body the heart of Perseus
and for those under the ground you loved
and those yet above, exact
what their bitter passion may desire; make
disaster a thing of blood inside the house;
wipe out the man stained with murder.

[*Enter Aegisthus.*]

AEGISTHUS

It is not without summons that I come, but called
by messenger, with news that there are strangers here
arrived, telling a story that brings no delight:

the death of Orestes. For our house, already bitten
and poisoned, to take this new load upon itself
would be a thing of dripping fear and blood. Yet how
shall I pass upon these rumors? As the living truth?
For messages made out of women's terror leap
high in the upward air and empty die. Do *you*
know anything of this by which to clear my mind?

CHORUS

We heard, yes. But go on inside and hear it from
the strangers. Messengers are never quite so sure
as a man's questions answered by the men themselves.

AEGISTHUS

I wish to question, carefully, this messenger
and learn if he himself was by when the man died
or if he heard but some blind rumor and so speaks.
The mind has eyes, not to be easily deceived.

[*Exit Aegisthus.*]

CHORUS

Zeus, Zeus, what shall I say, where make
a beginning of prayer for the gods' aid?
My will is good
but how shall I speak to match my need?
The bloody edges of the knives that rip
man-flesh are moving to work. It will mean
utter and final ruin imposed
on Agamemnon's
house: or our man will kindle a flame

and light of liberty, win the domain
and huge treasure again of his fathers.
Forlorn challenger, though blessed by God,
Orestes must come to grips with two,
so wrestle. Yet may he throw them.

[*A cry is heard from inside the house.*]

Listen, it goes
but how? What has been done in the house?
Stand we aside until the work is done, for so
we shall not seem to be accountable in this
foul business. For the fight is done, the issue drawn.

[*Enter a follower of Aegisthus.*]

FOLLOWER

O sorrow, all is sorrow for our stricken lord.
Raise up again a triple cry of sorrow, for
Aegisthus lives no longer. Open there, open
quick as you may, and slide back the doorbars on the
women's
gates. It will take the strength of a young arm, but not
to fight for one who is dead and done for. What use
there?
Ahoy!
My cry is to the deaf and I babble in vain
at sleepers to no purpose. Clytaemestra, where
is she, does what? Her neck is on the razor's edge
and ripe for lopping, as she did to others before.

[*Enter Clytaemestra.*]

CLYTAEMESTRA

What is this, and why are you shouting in the house?

FOLLOWER

I tell you, he is alive and killing the dead.

CLYTAEMESTRA

Ah, so. You speak in riddles, but I read the rhyme.
We have been won with the treachery by which we
slew.
Bring me quick, somebody, an ax to kill a man

[Exit follower.]

and we shall see if we can beat him before we
go down—so far gone are we in this wretched fight.

*[Enter Orestes and Pylades with
swords drawn.]*

ORESTES

You next: the other one in there has had enough.

CLYTAEMESTRA

Beloved, strong Aegisthus, are you dead indeed?

ORESTES

You love your man, then? You shall lie in the same
grave
with him, and never be unfaithful even in death.

CLYTAEMESTRA

Hold, my son. Oh take pity, child, before this breast
where many a time, a drowsing baby, you would feed

and with soft gums sucked in the milk that made you strong.

ORESTES

What shall I do, Pylades? Be shamed to kill my mother?

PYLADES

What then becomes thereafter of the oracles
declared by Loxias at Pytho? What of sworn oaths?
Count all men hateful to you rather than the gods.

ORESTES

I judge that you win. Your advice is good.

[*To Clytaemestra.*]

Come here.
My purpose is to kill you over his body.
You thought him bigger than my father while he lived.
Die then and sleep beside him, since he is the man
you love, and he you should have loved got only your
hate.

CLYTAEMESTRA

I raised you when you were little. May I grow old with you?

ORESTES

You killed my father. Would you make your home with me?

CLYTAEMESTRA

Destiny had some part in that, my child.

ORESTES

                                       Why then
destiny has so wrought that this shall be your death.

CLYTAEMESTRA

A mother has her curse, child. Are you not afraid?

ORESTES

No. You bore me and threw me away, to a hard life.

CLYTAEMESTRA

I sent you to a friend's house. This was no throwing away.

ORESTES

I was born of a free father. You sold me.

CLYTAEMESTRA

So? Where then is the price that I received for you?

ORESTES

I could say. It would be indecent to tell you.

CLYTAEMESTRA

Or if you do, tell also your father's vanities.

ORESTES

Blame him not. He suffered while you were sitting here at home.

CLYTAEMESTRA

It hurts women to be kept from their men, my child.

ORESTES

The man's hard work supports the women who sit at home.

CLYTAEMESTRA

I think, child, that you mean to kill your mother.

ORESTES

No.

It will be you who kill yourself. It will not be I.

CLYTAEMESTRA

Take care. Your mother's curse, like dogs, will drag you down.

ORESTES

How shall I escape my father's curse, if I fail here?

CLYTAEMESTRA

I feel like one who wastes live tears upon a tomb.

ORESTES

Yes, this is death, your wages for my father's fate.

CLYTAEMESTRA

You are the snake I gave birth to, and gave the breast.

ORESTES

Indeed, the terror of your dreams saw things to come clearly. You killed, and it was wrong. Now suffer wrong.

> *[Orestes and Pylades take Clytaemestra inside the house.]*

CHORUS

I have sorrow even for this pair in their twofold downfall. But since Orestes had the hardiness

to end this chain of bloodlettings, here lies our choice,
that the eyes' light in this house shall not utterly die.

Justice came at the last to Priam and all his sons
and it was heavy and hard,
but into the house of Agamemnon returned
the double lion, the double assault,
and the Pythian-steered exile
drove home to the hilt
vengeance, moving strongly in guidance sent by the
    god.

Raise up the high cry o over our lordships' house
won free of distress, free of its fortunes wasted
by two stained with murder,
free of its mournful luck.

He came back; his work lay in the secret attack
and it was stealthy and hard
but in the fighting his hand was steered by the very
    daughter
of Zeus: Right we call her,
mortals who speak of her and name her well. Her wind
is fury and death visited upon those she hates.

All that Loxias, who on Parnassus holds
the huge, the deep cleft in the ground, shrilled aloud,
by guile that is no guile
returns now to assault the wrong done and grown old.

Divinity keeps, we know not how, strength to resist
surrender to the wicked.
The power that holds the sky's majesty wins our
worship.

Light is here to behold.
The big bit that held our house is taken away.
Rise up, you halls, arise; for time grown too long
you lay tumbled along the ground.
Time brings all things to pass. Presently time shall
cross
the outgates of the house after the stain is driven
entire from the hearth
by ceremonies that wash clean and cast out the furies.
The dice of fortune shall be thrown once more, and lie
in a fair fall smiling
up at the new indwellers come to live in the house.

> [*The doors of the house open, to show*
> *Orestes standing over the bodies of*
> *Clytaemestra and Aegisthus. His*
> *attendants display the robe in which*
> *Clytaemestra had entangled Agamemnon*
> *and which she displayed after his murder.*]

ORESTES

Behold the twin tyrannies of our land, these two
who killed my father and who sacked my house. For a
time
they sat upon their thrones and kept their pride of
state,

and they are lovers still. So may you judge by what
befell them, for as they were pledged their oath abides.
They swore together death for my unhappy sire
and swore to die together. Now they keep their oath.

Behold again, o audience of these evil things,
the engine against my wretched father they devised,
the hands' entanglement, the hobbles for his feet.
Spread it out. Stand around me in a circle and
display this net that caught a man. So shall, not my
father, but that great father who sees all, the Sun,
look on my mother's sacrilegious handiwork
and be a witness for me in my day of trial
how it was in all right that I achieved this death,
my mother's: for of Aegisthus' death I take no count:
he has his seducer's punishment, no more than law.

But she, who plotted this foul death against the man
by whom she carried the weight of children underneath
her zone, burden once loved, shown hard and hateful
    now,
what does she seem to be? Some water snake, some
    viper
whose touch is rot even to him who felt no fang
strike, by that brutal and wrong daring in her heart.

And this thing: what shall I call it and be right, in all
eloquence? Trap for an animal or winding sheet
for dead man? Or bath curtain? Since it is a net,
robe you could call it, to entangle a man's feet.

Some highwayman might own a thing like this, to
  catch
the wayfarer and rob him of his money and
so make a living. With a treacherous thing like this
he could take many victims and go warm within.

May no such wife as she was come to live with me.
Sooner, let God destroy me, with no children born.

CHORUS

Ah, but the pitiful work.
Dismal the death that was your ending.
He is left alive; pain flowers for him.

ORESTES

Did she do it or did she not? My witness is
this great robe. It was thus she stained Aegisthus'
  sword.
Dip it and dip it again, the smear of blood conspires
with time to spoil the beauty of this precious thing.
Now I can praise him, now I can stand by to mourn
and speak before this web that killed my father; yet
I grieve for the thing done, the death, and all our race.
I have won; but my victory is soiled, and has no pride.

CHORUS

There is no mortal man who shall turn
unhurt his life's course to an end not marred.
There is trouble here. There is more to come.

ORESTES

I would have you know, I see not how this thing will
  end.

I am a charioteer whose course is wrenched outside
the track, for I am beaten, my rebellious senses
bolt with me headlong and the fear against my heart
is ready for the singing and dance of wrath. But while
I hold some grip still on my wits, I say publicly
to my friends: I killed my mother not without some
    right.
My father's murder stained her, and the gods' disgust.
As for the spells that charmed me to such daring, I
give you in chief the seer of Pytho, Loxias. He
declared I could do this and not be charged with wrong.
Of my evasion's punishment I will not speak:
no archery could hit such height of agony.
And look upon me now, how I go armored in
leafed branch and garland on my way to the centrestone
and sanctuary, and Apollo's level place,
the shining of the fabulous fire that never dies,
to escape this blood that is my own. Loxias ordained
that I should turn me to no other shrine than this.
To all men of Argos in time to come I say
they shall be witness, how these evil things were done.
I go, an outcast wanderer from this land, and leave
behind, in life, in death, the name of what I did.

CHORUS

No, what you did was well done. Do not therefore bind
your mouth to foul speech. Keep no evil on your lips.
You liberated all the Argive city when
you lopped the heads of these two snakes with one
    clean stroke.

ORESTES

No!
Women who serve this house, they come like gorgons,
  they
wear robes of black, and they are wreathed in a tangle
of snakes. I can no longer stay.

CHORUS

Orestes, dearest to your father of all men
what fancies whirl you? Hold, do not give way to fear.

ORESTES

These are no fancies of affliction. They are clear,
and real, and here; the bloodhounds of my mother's
  hate.

CHORUS

It is the blood still wet upon your hands, that makes
this shaken turbulence be thrown upon your sense.

ORESTES

Ah, Lord Apollo, how they grow and multiply,
repulsive for the blood drops of their dripping eyes.

CHORUS

There is one way to make you clean: let Loxias
touch you, and set you free from these disturbances.

ORESTES

You can not see them, but I see them. I am driven
from this place. I can stay here no longer.

[*Exit.*]

CHORUS

Good luck go with you then, and may the god look on
you with favor and guard you in kind circumstance.

Here on this house of the kings the third
storm has broken, with wind
from the inward race, and gone its course.
The children were eaten: there was the first
affliction, the curse of Thyestes.
Next came the royal death, when a man
and lord of Achaean armies went down
killed in the bath. Third
is for the savior. He came. Shall I call
it that, or death? Where
is the end? Where shall the fury of fate
be stilled to sleep, be done with?

[*Exeunt.*]

THE EUMENIDES

CHARACTERS

PRIESTESS OF APOLLO, THE PYTHIA

APOLLO

HERMES (SILENT)

GHOST OF CLYTAEMESTRA

ORESTES

ATHENE

CHORUS OF EUMENIDES (FURIES)

SECOND CHORUS; WOMEN OF ATHENS

JURYMEN, HERALD, CITIZENS OF ATHENS
(ALL SILENT PARTS)

THE EUMENIDES

SCENE: *Delphi, before the sanctuary of Pythian Apollo.*

[Enter, alone, the Pythia.]

PYTHIA

I give first place of honor in my prayer to her
who of the gods first prophesied, the Earth; and next
to Themis, who succeeded to her mother's place
of prophecy; so runs the legend; and in third
succession, given by free consent, not won by force,
another Titan daughter of Earth was seated here.
This was Phoebe. She gave it as a birthday gift
to Phoebus, who is called still after Phoebe's name.
And he, leaving the pond of Delos and the reef,
grounded his ship at the roadstead of Pallas, then
made his way to this land and a Parnassian home.
Deep in respect for his degree Hephaestus' sons
conveyed him here, for these are builders of roads, and
    changed
the wilderness to a land that was no wilderness.
He came so, and the people highly honored him,
with Delphus, lord and helmsman of the country. Zeus
made his mind full with godship and prophetic craft
and placed him, fourth in a line of seers, upon this
    throne.
So, Loxias is the spokesman of his father, Zeus.
These are the gods I set in the proem of my prayer.

But Pallas-before-the-temple has her right in all
I say. I worship the nymphs where the Corycian rock
is hollowed inward, haunt of birds and paced by gods.
Bromius, whom I forget not, sways this place. From
    here
in divine form he led his Bacchanals in arms
to hunt down Pentheus like a hare in the deathtrap.
I call upon the springs of Pleistus, on the power
of Poseidon, and on final loftiest Zeus,
then go to sit in prophecy on the throne. May all
grant me that this of all my entrances shall be
the best by far. If there are any Hellenes here
let them draw lots, so enter, as the custom is.
My prophecy is only as the god may guide.

> [*She enters the temple and almost*
> *immediately comes out again.*]

Things terrible to tell and for the eyes to see
terrible drove me out again from Loxias' house
so that I have no strength and cannot stand on
    springing
feet, but run with hands' help and my legs have no
    speed.
An old woman afraid is nothing: a child, no more.
    See, I am on my way to the wreath-hung recess
and on the centrestone I see a man with god's
defilement on him postured in the suppliant's seat
with blood dripping from his hands and from a
    new-drawn sword,
holding too a branch that had grown high on an olive

tree, decorously wrapped in a great tuft of wool,
and the fleece shone. So far, at least, I can speak clear.
  In front of this man slept a startling company
of women lying all upon the chairs. Or not
women, I think I call them rather gorgons, only
not gorgons either, since their shape is not the same.
I saw some creatures painted in a picture once,
who tore the food from Phineus, only these had no
wings, that could be seen; they are black and utterly
repulsive, and they snore with breath that drives one
    back.
From their eyes drips the foul ooze, and their dress is
    such
as is not right to wear in the presence of the gods'
statues, nor even into any human house.
I have never seen the tribe that owns this company
nor know what piece of earth can claim with pride it
    bore
such brood, and without hurt and tears for labor given.
  Now after this the master of the house must take
his own measures: Apollo Loxias, who is very strong
and heals by divination; reads portentous signs,
and so clears out the houses others hold as well.

> [*Exit. The doors of the temple open and
> show Orestes surrounded by the sleeping
> Furies, Apollo and Hermes beside him.*]

APOLLO

I will not give you up. Through to the end standing
your guardian, whether by your side or far away,

I shall not weaken toward your enemies. See now
how I have caught and overpowered these lewd
   creatures.
The repulsive maidens have been stilled to sleep, those
   gray
and aged children, they with whom no mortal man,
no god, nor even any beast, will have to do.
It was because of evil they were born, because
they hold the evil darkness of the Pit below
Earth, loathed alike by men and by the heavenly gods.
Nevertheless, run from them, never weaken. They
will track you down as you stride on across the long
land, and your driven feet forever pound the earth,
on across the main water and the circle-washed
cities. Be herdsman to this hard march. Never fail
until you come at last to Pallas' citadel.
Kneel there, and clasp the ancient idol in your arms,
and there we shall find those who will judge this case,
   and words
to say that will have the magic in their figures. Thus
you will be rid of your afflictions, once for all.
For it was I who made you strike your mother down.

ORESTES

My lord Apollo, you understand what it means to do
no wrong. Learn also what it is not to neglect.
None can mistrust your power to do good, if you will.

APOLLO

Remember: the fear must not give you a beaten heart.
Hermes, you are my brother from a single sire.

Look after him, and as you are named the god who
   guides,
be such in strong fact. He is my suppliant. Shepherd
   him
with fortunate escort on his journeys among men.
The wanderer has rights which Zeus acknowledges.

   [*Exit Apollo, then Orestes guided by Hermes.*
                Enter the ghost of Clytaemestra.]

CLYTAEMESTRA

You would sleep, then? And what use are you, if you
   sleep?
It is because of you I go dishonored thus
among the rest of the dead. Because of those I killed
my bad name among the perished suffers no eclipse
but I am driven in disgrace. I say to you
that I am charged with guilt most grave by these. And
   yet
I suffered too, horribly, and from those most dear,
yet none among the powers is angered for my sake
that I was slaughtered, and by matricidal hands.
Look at these gashes in my heart, think where they
   came
from. Eyes illuminate the sleeping brain,
but in the daylight man's future cannot be seen.
   Yet I have given you much to lap up, outpourings
without wine, sober propitiations, sacrificed
in secrecy of night and on a hearth of fire
for you, at an hour given to no other god.
Now I watch all these honors trampled into the ground,

and he is out and gone away like any fawn
so lightly, from the very middle of your nets,
sprung clear, and laughing merrily at you. Hear me.
It is my life depends upon this spoken plea.
Think then, o goddesses beneath the ground. For I,
the dream of Clytaemestra, call upon your name.

[*The Furies stir in their sleep and whimper.*]

CLYTAEMESTRA

Oh, whimper, then, but your man has got away and
    gone
far. He has friends to help him, who are not like mine.

[*They whimper again.*]

CLYTAEMESTRA

Too much sleep and no pity for my plight. I stand,
his mother, here, killed by Orestes. He is gone.

[*They moan in their sleep.*]

CLYTAEMESTRA

You moan, you sleep. Get on your feet quickly, will
    you?
What have you yet got done, except to do evil?

[*They moan again.*]

CLYTAEMESTRA

Sleep and fatigue, two masterful conspirators,
have dimmed the deadly anger of the mother-snake.

[*The Chorus start violently, then speak in
                        their sleep.*]

CHORUS

Get him, get him, get him, get him. Make sure.

CLYTAEMESTRA

The beast you are after is a dream, but like the hound
whose thought of hunting has no lapse, you bay him
    on.
What are you about? Up, let not work's weariness
beat you, nor slacken with sleep so you forget my pain.
Scold your own heart and hurt it, as it well deserves,
for this is discipline's spur upon her own. Let go
upon this man the stormblasts of your bloodshot
    breath,
wither him in your wind, after him, hunt him down
once more, and shrivel him in your vitals' heat and
    flame.

> [*The ghost disappears, and the Chorus*
> *waken and, as they waken, speak severally.*]

CHORUS

Waken. You are awake, wake her, as I did you.
You dream still? On your feet and kick your sleep
    aside.
Let us see whether this morning-song means vanity.

> [*Here they begin to howl.*]

Sisters, we have had wrong done us.
When I have undergone so much and all in vain.
Suffering, suffering, bitter, oh shame shame,
unendurable wrong.

The hunted beast has slipped clean from our nets and
   gone.
Sleep won me, and I lost my capture.

Shame, son of Zeus! Robber is all you are.
A young god, you have ridden down powers gray with
   age,
taken the suppliant, though a godless man, who hurt
the mother who gave him birth.
Yourself a god, you stole the matricide away.
Where in this act shall any man say there is right?

The accusation came upon me from my dreams,
and hit me, as with goad in the mid-grip of his fist
the charioteer strikes,
but deep, beneath lobe and heart.
The executioner's cutting whip is mine to feel
and the weight of pain is big, heavy to bear.

Such are the actions of the younger gods. These hold
by unconditional force, beyond all right, a throne
that runs reeking blood,
blood at the feet, blood at the head.
The very stone centre of earth here in our eyes horrible
with blood and curse stands plain to see.

Himself divine, he has spoiled his secret shrine's
hearth with the stain, driven and hallooed the action
   on.

He made man's way cross the place of the ways of god
and blighted age-old distributions of power.
He has wounded me, but he shall not get this man
  away.
Let him hide under the ground, he shall never go free.
Cursed suppliant, he shall feel against his head
another murderer rising out of the same seed.

[*Apollo enters again from his sanctuary.*]

APOLLO

Get out, I tell you, go and leave this house. Away
in haste, from your presence set the mantic chamber
  free,
else you may feel the flash and bite of a flying snake
launched from the twisted thong of gold that spans my
  bow
to make you in your pain spew out the black and
  foaming
blood of men, vomit the clots sucked from their veins.
This house is no right place for such as you to cling
upon; but where, by judgment given, heads are lopped
and eyes gouged out, throats cut, and by the spoil of sex
the glory of young boys is defeated, where mutilation
lives, and stoning, and the long moan of tortured men
spiked underneath the spine and stuck on pales. Listen
to how the gods spit out the manner of that feast
your loves lean to. The whole cast of your shape is
  guide
to what you are, the like of whom should hole in the
  cave

of the blood-reeking lion, not in oracular
interiors, like mine nearby, wipe off your filth.
Out then, you flock of goats without a herdsman, since
no god has such affection as to tend this brood.

CHORUS

My lord Apollo, it is your turn to listen now.
Your own part in this is more than accessory.
You are the one who did it; all the guilt is yours.

APOLLO

So? How? Continue speaking, until I understand.

CHORUS

You gave this outlander the word to kill his mother.

APOLLO

The word to exact price for his father. What of that?

CHORUS

You then dared take him in, fresh from his bloodletting.

APOLLO

Yes, and I told him to take refuge in this house.

CHORUS

You are abusive then to those who sped him here?

APOLLO

Yes. It was not for you to come near this house;

CHORUS

                                   and yet
we have our duty. It was to do what we have done.

APOLLO

An office? You? Sound forth your glorious privilege.

CHORUS

This: to drive matricides out of their houses.

APOLLO

Then
what if it be the woman and she kills her man?

CHORUS

Such murder would not be the shedding of kindred
blood.

APOLLO

You have made into a thing of no account, no place,
the sworn faith of Zeus and of Hera, lady
of consummations, and Cypris by such argument
is thrown away, outlawed, and yet the sweetest things
in man's life come from her, for married love between
man and woman is bigger than oaths, guarded by right
of nature. If when such kill each other you relent
so as not to take vengeance nor eye them in wrath,
then I deny your manhunt of Orestes goes
with right. I see that one cause moves you to strong
rage
but on the other clearly you are unmoved to act.
Pallas divine shall review the pleadings of this case.

CHORUS

Nothing will ever make me let that man go free.

APOLLO

Keep after him then, and make more trouble for
yourselves.

CHORUS

Do not try to dock my privilege by argument.

APOLLO

I would not take your privilege if you gave it me.

CHORUS

No, for you are called great beside the throne of Zeus
already, but the motherblood drives me, and I go
to win my right upon this man and hunt him down.

APOLLO

But I shall give the suppliant help and rescue, for
if I willingly fail him who turns to me for aid,
his wrath, before gods and men, is a fearful thing.

[*They go out, separately. The scene is now
Athens, on the Acropolis before the
temple and statue of Athene. Orestes enters
and takes suppliant posture at the feet
of the statue.*]

ORESTES

My lady Athene, it is at Loxias' behest
I come. Then take in of your grace the wanderer
who comes, no suppliant, not unwashed of hand, but
one

blunted at last, and worn and battered on the outland
habitations and the beaten ways of men.
Crossing the dry land and the sea alike, keeping
the ordinances of Apollo's oracle
I come, goddess, before your statue and your house
to keep watch here and wait the issue of my trial.

> [*The Chorus enter severally, looking for*
> *Orestes.*]

CHORUS

So. Here the man has left a clear trail behind; keep on,
keep on, as the unspeaking accuser tells us, by
whose sense, like hounds after a bleeding fawn, we trail
our quarry by the splash and drip of blood. And now
my lungs are blown with abundant and with wearisome
work, mankilling. My range has been the entire extent
of land, and, flown unwinged across the open water,
I am here, and give way to no ship in my pursuit.
Our man has gone to cover somewhere in this place.
The welcome smell of human blood has told me so.

Look again, look again,
search everywhere, let
not the matricide
steal away and escape.

> [*They see Orestes.*]

See there! He clings to defence
again, his arms winding the immortal goddess'
image, so tries to be quit out of our hands.

THE EUMENIDES · 149

It shall not be. His mother's blood spilled on the ground
can not come back again.
It is all soaked and drained into the ground and gone.

You must give back for her blood from the living man
red blood of your body to suck, and from your own
I could feed, with bitter-swallowed drench,
turn your strength limp while yet you live and drag you
    down
where you must pay for the pain of the murdered
    mother,
and watch the rest of the mortals stained with violence
against god or guest
or hurt parents who were close and dear,
each with the pain upon him that his crime deserves.
Hades is great, Hades calls men to reckoning
there under the ground,
sees all, and cuts it deep in his recording mind.

ORESTES

I have been beaten and been taught, I understand
the many rules of absolution, where it is right
to speak and where be silent. In this action now
speech has been ordered by my teacher, who is wise.
The stain of blood dulls now and fades upon my hand.
My blot of matricide is being washed away.
When it was fresh still, at the hearth of the god,
    Phoebus,
this was absolved and driven out by sacrifice
of swine, and the list were long if I went back to tell
of all I met who were not hurt by being with me.

Time in his aging overtakes all things alike.
Now it is from pure mouth and with good auspices
I call upon Athene, queen of this land, to come
and rescue me. She, without work of her spear, shall
    win
myself and all my land and all the Argive host
to stand her staunch companion for the rest of time.
Whether now ranging somewhere in the Libyan land
beside her father's crossing and by Triton's run
of waters she sets upright or enshrouded foot
rescuing there her friends, or on the Phlegraean flat
like some bold man of armies sweeps with eyes the
    scene,
let her come! She is a god and hears me far away.
So may she set me free from what is at my back.

CHORUS

Neither Apollo nor Athene's strength must win
you free, save you from going down forgotten, without
knowing where joy lies anywhere inside your heart,
blood drained, chewed dry by the powers of death, a
    wraith, a shell.
You will not speak to answer, spew my challenge
    away?
You are consecrate to me and fattened for my feast,
and you shall feed me while you live, not cut down
    first
at the altar. Hear the spell I sing to bind you in.

Come then, link we our choral. Ours
to show forth the power

and terror of our music, declare
our rights of office, how we conspire
to steer men's lives.
We hold we are straight and just. If a man
can spread his hands and show they are clean,
no wrath of ours shall lurk for him.
Unscathed he walks through his life time.
But one like this man before us, with stained
hidden hands, and the guilt upon him,
shall find us beside him, as witnesses
of the truth, and we show clear in the end
to avenge the blood of the murdered.

Mother, o my mother night, who gave me
birth, to be a vengeance on the seeing
and the blind, hear me. For Leto's
youngling takes my right away,
stealing from my clutch the prey
that crouches, whose blood would wipe
at last the motherblood away.

Over the beast doomed to the fire
this is the chant, scatter of wits,
frenzy and fear, hurting the heart,
song of the Furies
binding brain and blighting blood
in its stringless melody.

This the purpose that the all-involving
destiny spun, to be ours and to be shaken

never: when mortals assume outrage
of own hand in violence,
these we dog, till one goes
under earth. Nor does death
set them altogether free.

Over the beast doomed to the fire
this is the chant, scatter of wits,
frenzy and fear, hurting the heart,
song of the Furies
binding brain and blighting blood
in its stringless melody.

When we were born such lots were assigned for our
    keeping.
So the immortals must hold hands off, nor is there
one who shall sit at our feasting.
For sheer white robes I have no right and no portion.

I have chosen overthrow
of houses, where the Battlegod
grown within strikes near and dear
down. So we swoop upon this man
here. He is strong, but we wear him down
for the blood that is still wet on him.

Here we stand in our haste to wrench from all others
these devisings, make the gods clear of our counsels
so that even appeal comes

not to them, since Zeus has ruled our blood dripping
  company
outcast, nor will deal with us.

I have chosen overthrow
of houses, where the Battlegod
grown within strikes near and dear
down. So we swoop upon this man
here. He is strong, but we wear him down
for the blood that is still wet on him.

Men's illusions in their pride under the sky melt
down, and are diminished into the ground, gone
before the onset of our black robes, pulsing
of our vindictive feet against them.
For with a long leap from high
above and dead drop of weight
I bring foot's force crashing down
to cut the legs from under even
the runner, and spill him to ruin.

He falls, and does not know in the daze of his folly.
Such in the dark of man is the mist of infection
that hovers, and moaning rumor tells how his house
  lies
under fog that glooms above.

For with a long leap from high
above, and dead drop of weight,
I bring foot's force crashing down

to cut the legs from under even
the runner, and spill him to ruin.

All holds. For we are strong and skilled;
we have authority; we hold
memory of evil; we are stern
nor can men's pleadings bend us. We
drive through our duties, spurned, outcast
from gods, driven apart to stand in light
not of the sun. So sheer with rock are ways
for those who see, as upon those whose eyes are lost.

Is there a man who does not fear
this, does not shrink to hear
how my place has been ordained,
granted and given by destiny
and god, absolute? Privilege
primeval yet is mine, nor am I without place
though it be underneath the ground
and in no sunlight and in gloom that I must stand.

[*Athene enters, in full armor.*]

ATHENE

From far away I heard the outcry of your call.
It was beside Scamandrus. I was taking seisin
of land, for there the Achaean lords of war and first
fighters gave me large portion of all their spears
had won, the land root and stock to be mine for all
eternity, for the sons of Theseus a choice gift.
From there, sped on my weariless feet, I came, wingless

but in the rush and speed of the aegis fold. And now
I see upon this land a novel company
which, though it brings no terror to my eyes, brings
    still
wonder. Who are you? I address you all alike,
both you, the stranger kneeling at my image here,
and you, who are like no seed ever begotten, not
seen ever by the gods as goddesses, nor yet
stamped in the likenesses of any human form.
But no. This is the place of the just. Its rights forbid
even the innocent to speak evil of his mates.

CHORUS

Daughter of Zeus, you shall hear all compressed to brief
measure. We are the gloomy children of the night.
Curses they call us in our homes beneath the ground.

ATHENE

I know your race, then, and the names by which you
    are called.

CHORUS

You shall be told of our position presently.

ATHENE

I can know that, if one will give me a clear account.

CHORUS

We drive from home those who have shed the blood of
    men.

ATHENE

Where is the place, then, where the killer's flight shall
    end?

CHORUS

A place where happiness is nevermore allowed.

ATHENE

Is he one? Do you blast him to this kind of flight?

CHORUS

Yes. He murdered his mother by deliberate choice.

ATHENE

By random force, or was it fear of someone's wrath?

CHORUS

Where is the spur to justify man's matricide?

ATHENE

Here are two sides, and only half the argument.

CHORUS

He is unwilling to give or to accept an oath.

ATHENE

You wish to be called righteous rather than act right.

CHORUS

No. How so? Out of the riches of your wit, explain.

ATHENE

I say, wrong must not win by technicalities.

CHORUS

Examine him then yourself. Decide it, and be fair.

ATHENE

You would turn over authority in this case to me?

CHORUS

By all means. Your father's degree, and yours, deserve
as much.

ATHENE

Your turn, stranger. What will you say in answer?
Speak,
tell me your country and your birth, what has befallen
you, then defend yourself against the anger of these;
if it was confidence in the right that made you sit
to keep this image near my hearth, a supplicant
in the tradition of Ixion, sacrosanct.
Give me an answer which is plain to understand.

ORESTES

Lady Athene, first I will take the difficult thought
away that lies in these last words you spoke. I am
no supplicant, nor was it because I had a stain
upon my hand that I sat at your image. I
will give you a strong proof that what I say is true.
It is the law that the man of the bloody hand must
speak
no word until, by action of one who can cleanse,
blood from a young victim has washed his blood away.
Long since, at the homes of others, I have been
absolved
thus, both by running waters and by victims slain.

I count this scruple now out of the way. Learn next
with no delay where I am from. I am of Argos
and it is to my honor that you ask the name

of my father, Agamemnon, lord of seafarers,
and your companion when you made the Trojan city
of Ilium no city any more. He died
without honor when he came home. It was my mother
of the dark heart, who entangled him in subtle gyves
and cut him down. The bath is witness to his death.
I was an exile in the time before this. I came back
and killed the woman who gave me birth. I plead
  guilty.
My father was dear, and this was vengeance for his
  blood.
Apollo shares responsibility for this.
He counterspurred my heart and told me of pains to
  come
if I should fail to act against the guilty ones.
This is my case. Decide if it be right or wrong.
I am in your hands. Where my fate falls, I shall accept.

ATHENE

The matter is too big for any mortal man
who thinks he can judge it. Even I have not the right
to analyse cases of murder where wrath's edge
is sharp, and all the more since you have come, and
  clung
a clean and innocent supplicant, against my doors.
You bring no harm to my city. I respect your rights.
Yet these, too, have their work. We cannot brush them
  aside,
and if this action so runs that they fail to win,
the venom of their resolution will return

to infect the soil, and sicken all my land to death.
Here is dilemma. Whether I let them stay or drive
them off, it is a hard course and will hurt. Then, since
the burden of the case is here, and rests on me,
I shall select judges of manslaughter, and swear
them in, establish a court into all time to come.

Litigants, call your witnesses, have ready your proofs
as evidence under bond to keep this case secure.
I will pick the finest of my citizens, and come
back. They shall swear to make no judgment that is not
just, and make clear where in this action the truth lies.

[*Exit.*]

CHORUS

Here is overthrow of all
the young laws, if the claim
of this matricide shall stand
good, his crime be sustained.
Should this be, every man will find a way
to act at his own caprice;
over and over again in time
to come, parents shall await
the deathstroke at their children's hands.

We are the Angry Ones. But we
shall watch no more over works
of men, and so act. We shall
let loose indiscriminate death.
Man shall learn from man's lot, forejudge

the evils of his neighbor's case,
see respite and windfall in storm:
pathetic prophet who consoles
with strengthless cures, in vain.
Nevermore let one who feels
the stroke of accident, uplift
his voice and make outcry, thus:
"Oh Justice!
Throned powers of the Furies, help!"
Such might be the pitiful cry
of some father, of the stricken
mother, their appeal. Now
the House of Justice has collapsed.

There are times when fear is good.
It must keep its watchful place
at the heart's controls. There is
advantage
in the wisdom won from pain.
Should the city, should the man
rear a heart that nowhere goes
in fear, how shall such a one
any more respect the right?

Refuse the life of anarchy;
refuse the life devoted to
one master.
The in-between has the power
by God's grant always, though
his ordinances vary.

I will speak in defence
of reason: for the very child
of vanity is violence;
but out of health
in the heart issues the beloved
and the longed-for, prosperity.

All for all I say to you:
bow before the altar of right.
You shall not
eye advantage, and heel
it over with foot of force.
Vengeance will be upon you.
The all is bigger than you.
Let man see this and take
care, to mother and father,
and to the guest
in the gates welcomed, give all rights
that befall their position.

The man who does right, free-willed, without
    constraint
shall not lose happiness
nor be wiped out with all his generation.
But the transgressor, I tell you, the bold man
who brings in confusion of goods unrightly won,
at long last and perforce, when ship toils
under tempest must strike his sail
in the wreck of his rigging.

He calls on those who hear not, caught inside
the hard wrestle of water.
The spirit laughs at the hot hearted man,
the man who said "never to me," watches him
pinned in distress, unable to run free of the crests.
He had good luck in his life. Now
he smashes it on the reef of Right
and drowns, unwept and forgotten.

[*Athene re-enters, guiding twelve citizens
chosen as jurors and attended by a herald.
Other citizens follow.*]

ATHENE

Herald, make proclamation and hold in the host
assembled. Let the stabbing voice of the Etruscan
trumpet, blown to the full with mortal wind, crash out
its high call to all the assembled populace.
For in the filling of this senatorial ground
it is best for all the city to be silent and learn
the measures I have laid down into the rest of time.
So too these litigants, that their case be fairly tried.

[*Trumpet call. All take their places.
Enter Apollo.*]

CHORUS

My lord Apollo, rule within your own domain.
What in this matter has to do with you? Declare.

APOLLO

I come to testify. This man, by observed law,

THE EUMENIDES · 163

came to me as suppliant, took his place by hearth and
   hall,
and it was I who cleaned him of the stain of blood.
I have also come to help him win his case. I bear
responsibility for his mother's murder.

> [*To Athene.*]
>   You
who know the rules, initiate the trial. Preside.

ATHENE [*to the Furies*]

   I declare the trial opened. Yours is the first word.
   For it must justly be the pursuer who speaks first
   and opens the case, and makes plain what the action is.

CHORUS

   We are many, but we shall cut it short. You, then,
   word against word answer our charges one by one.
   Say first, did you kill your mother or did you not?

ORESTES

   Yes, I killed her. There shall be no denial of that.

CHORUS

   There are three falls in the match and one has gone to
      us.

ORESTES

   So you say. But you have not even thrown your man.

CHORUS

   So. Then how did you kill her? You are bound to say.

ORESTES

I do. With drawn sword in my hand I cut her throat.

CHORUS

By whose persuasion and advice did you do this?

ORESTES

By order of this god, here. So he testifies.

CHORUS

The Prophet guided you into this matricide?

ORESTES

Yes. I have never complained of this. I do not now.

CHORUS

When sentence seizes you, you will talk a different
way.

ORESTES

I have no fear. My father will aid me from the grave.

CHORUS

Kill your mother, then put trust in a corpse! Trust on.

ORESTES

Yes. She was dirtied twice over with disgrace.

CHORUS

Tell me how, and explain it to the judges here.

ORESTES

She murdered her husband, and thereby my father too.

CHORUS

Of this stain, death has set her free. But you still live.

ORESTES

When she lived, why did you not descend and drive her
out?

CHORUS

The man she killed was not of blood congenital.

ORESTES

But am I then involved with my mother by blood-bond?

CHORUS

Murderer, yes. How else could she have nursed you
beneath
her heart? Do you forswear your mother's intimate
blood?

ORESTES

Yours to bear witness now, Apollo, and expound
the case for me, if I was right to cut her down.
I will not deny I did this thing, because I did
do it. But was the bloodshed right or not? Decide
and answer. As you answer, I shall state my case.

APOLLO

To you, established by Athene in your power,
I shall speak justly. I am a prophet, I shall not
lie. Never, for man, woman, nor city, from my throne
of prophecy have I spoken a word, except
that which Zeus, father of Olympians, might command.

This is justice. Recognize then how great its strength.
I tell you, follow our father's will. For not even
the oath that binds you is more strong than Zeus is
    strong.

CHORUS

Then Zeus, as you say, authorized the oracle
to this Orestes, stating he could wreak the death
of his father on his mother, and it would have no force?

APOLLO

It is not the same thing for a man of blood to die
honored with the king's staff given by the hand of god,
and that by means of a woman, not with the far cast
of fierce arrows, as an Amazon might have done,
but in a way that you shall hear, o Pallas and you
who sit in state to judge this action by your vote.

He had come home from his campaigning. He had done
better than worse, in the eyes of a fair judge. She lay
in wait for him. It was the bath. When he was at
its edge, she hooded the robe on him, and in the blind
and complex toils tangled her man, and chopped him
    down.

There is the story of the death of a great man,
solemn in all men's sight, lord of the host of ships.
I have called the woman what she was, so that the
    people
whose duty it is to try this case may be inflamed.

CHORUS

Zeus, by your story, gives first place to the father's
  death.
Yet Zeus himself shackled elder Cronus, his own
father. Is this not contradiction? I testify,
judges, that this is being said in your hearing.

APOLLO

You foul animals, from whom the gods turn in disgust,
Zeus could undo shackles, such hurt can be made good,
and there is every kind of way to get out. But once
the dust has drained down all a man's blood, once the
  man
has died, there is no raising of him up again.
This is a thing for which my father never made
curative spells. All other states, without effort
of hard breath, he can completely rearrange.

CHORUS

See what it means to force acquittal of this man.
He has spilled his mother's blood upon the ground.
  Shall he
then be at home in Argos in his father's house?
What altars of the community shall he use? Is there
a brotherhood's lustration that will let him in?

APOLLO

I will tell you, and I will answer correctly. Watch.
The mother is no parent of that which is called
her child, but only nurse of the new-planted seed

that grows. The parent is he who mounts. A stranger
    she
preserves a stranger's seed, if no god interfere.
I will show you proof of what I have explained. There
    can
be a father without any mother. There she stands,
the living witness, daughter of Olympian Zeus,
she who was never fostered in the dark of the womb
yet such a child as no goddess could bring to birth.
In all else, Pallas, as I best may understand,
I shall make great your city and its populace.
So I have brought this man to sit beside the hearth
of your house, to be your true friend for the rest of
    time,
so you shall win him, goddess, to fight by your side,
and among men to come this shall stand a strong bond
that his and your own people's children shall be friends.

ATHENE

Shall I assume that enough has now been said, and tell
the judges to render what they believe a true verdict?

CHORUS

Every arrow we had has been shot now. We wait
on their decision, to see how the case has gone.

ATHENE

So then. How shall I act correctly in your eyes?

APOLLO

You have heard what you have heard, and as you cast
    your votes,

good friends, respect in your hearts the oath that you
have sworn.

ATHENE

If it please you, men of Attica, hear my decree
now, on this first case of bloodletting I have judged.
For Aegeus' population, this forevermore
shall be the ground where justices deliberate.
Here is the Hill of Ares, here the Amazons
encamped and built their shelters when they came in
    arms
for spite of Theseus, here they piled their rival towers
to rise, new city, and dare his city long ago,
and slew their beasts for Ares. So this rock is named
from then the Hill of Ares. Here the reverence
of citizens, their fear and kindred do-no-wrong
shall hold by day and in the blessing of night alike
all while the people do not muddy their own laws
with foul infusions. But if bright water you stain
with mud, you nevermore will find it fit to drink.
No anarchy, no rule of a single master. Thus
I advise my citizens to govern and to grace,
and not to cast fear utterly from your city. What
man who fears nothing at all is ever righteous? Such
be your just terrors, and you may deserve and have
salvation for your citadel, your land's defence,
such as is nowhere else found among men, neither
among the Scythians, nor the land that Pelops held.
I establish this tribunal. It shall be untouched
by money-making, grave but quick to wrath, watchful
to protect those who sleep, a sentry on the land.

These words I have unreeled are for my citizens,
advice into the future. All must stand upright
now, take each man his ballot in his hand, think on
his oath, and make his judgment. For my word is said.

CHORUS

I give you counsel by no means to disregard
this company. We can be a weight to crush your land.

APOLLO

I speak too. I command you to fear, and not
make void the yield of oracles from Zeus and me.

CHORUS

You honor bloody actions where you have no right.
The oracles you give shall be no longer clean.

APOLLO

My father's purposes are twisted then. For he
was appealed to by Ixion, the first murderer.

CHORUS

Talk! But for my part, if I do not win the case,
I shall come back to this land and it will feel my
    weight.

APOLLO

Neither among the elder nor the younger gods
have you consideration. I shall win this suit.

CHORUS

Such was your action in the house of Pheres. Then
you beguiled the Fates to let mortals go free from death.

APOLLO

Is it not right to do well by the man who shows
you worship, and above all when he stands in need?

CHORUS

You won the ancient goddesses over with wine
and so destroyed the orders of an elder time.

APOLLO

You shall not win the issue of this suit, but shall
be made to void your poison to no enemy's hurt.

CHORUS

Since you, a young god, would ride down my elder age,
I must stay here and listen to how the trial goes,
being yet uncertain to loose my anger on the state.

ATHENE

It is my task to render final judgment here.
This is a ballot for Orestes I shall cast.
There is no mother anywhere who gave me birth,
and, but for marriage, I am always for the male
with all my heart, and strongly on my father's side.
So, in a case where the wife has killed her husband,
  lord
of the house, her death shall not mean most to me. And
  if
the other votes are even, then Orestes wins.
You of the jurymen who have this duty assigned,
shake out the ballots from the vessels, with all speed.

ORESTES

Phoebus Apollo, what will the decision be?

CHORUS

Darkness of night, our mother, are you here to watch?

ORESTES

This is the end for me. The noose, or else the light.

CHORUS

Here our destruction, or our high duties confirmed.

APOLLO

Shake out the votes accurately, Athenian friends.
Be careful as you pick them up. Make no mistake.
In the lapse of judgment great disaster comes. The cast
of a single ballot has restored a house entire.

ATHENE

The man before us has escaped the charge of blood.
The ballots are in equal number for each side.

ORESTES

Pallas Athene, you have kept my house alive.
When I had lost the land of my fathers you gave me
a place to live. Among the Hellenes they shall say:
"A man of Argos lives again in the estates
of his father, all by grace of Pallas Athene, and
Apollo, and with them the all-ordaining god
the Savior"—who remembers my father's death, who
    looked
upon my mother's advocates, and rescues me.
I shall go home now, but before I go I swear
to this your country and to this your multitude
of people into all the bigness of time to be,

that never man who holds the helm of my state shall
   come
against your country in the ordered strength of spears,
but though I lie then in my grave, I still shall wreak
helpless bad luck and misadventure upon all
who stride across the oath that I have sworn: their
   ways
disconsolate make, their crossings full of evil
augury, so they shall be sorry that they moved.
But while they keep the upright way, and hold in high
regard the city of Pallas, and align their spears
to fight beside her, I shall be their gracious spirit.
And so farewell, you and your city's populace.
May you outwrestle and overthrow all those who come
against you, to your safety and your spears' success.

> [*Exit. Exit also Apollo.*]

CHORUS

Gods of the younger generation, you have ridden down
the laws of the elder time, torn them out of my hands.
I, disinherited, suffering, heavy with anger
shall let loose on the land
the vindictive poison
dripping deadly out of my heart upon the ground;
this from itself shall breed
cancer, the leafless, the barren
to strike, for the right, their low lands
and drag its smear of mortal infection on the ground.
What shall I do? Afflicted
I am mocked by these people.

I have borne what can not
be borne. Great the sorrows and the dishonor upon
the sad daughters of night.

ATHENE

Listen to me. I would not have you be so grieved.
For you have not been beaten. This was the result
of a fair ballot which was even. You were not
dishonored, but the luminous evidence of Zeus
was there, and he who spoke the oracle was he
who ordered Orestes so to act and not be hurt.
Do not be angry any longer with this land
nor bring the bulk of your hatred down on it, do not
render it barren of fruit, nor spill the dripping rain
of death in fierce and jagged lines to eat the seeds.
In complete honesty I promise you a place
of your own, deep hidden under ground that is yours by
     right
where you shall sit on shining chairs beside the hearth
to accept devotions offered by your citizens.

CHORUS

Gods of the younger generation, you have ridden down
the laws of the elder time, torn them out of my hands.
I, disinherited, suffering, heavy with anger
shall let loose on the land
the vindictive poison
dripping deadly out of my heart upon the ground;
this from itself shall breed
cancer, the leafless, the barren
to strike, for the right, their low lands

and drag its smear of mortal infection on the ground.
What shall I do? Afflicted
I am mocked by these people.
I have borne what can not
be borne. Great the sorrow and the dishonor upon
the sad daughters of night.

ATHENE

No, not dishonored. You are goddesses. Do not
in too much anger make this place of mortal men
uninhabitable. I have Zeus behind me. Do
we need to speak of that? I am the only god
who know the keys to where his thunderbolts are
    locked.
We do not need such, do we? Be reasonable
and do not from a reckless mouth cast on the land
spells that will ruin every thing which might bear fruit.
No. Put to sleep the bitter strength in the black wave
and live with me and share my pride of worship. Here
is a big land, and from it you shall win first fruits
in offerings for children and the marriage rite
for always. Then you will say my argument was good.

CHORUS

That they could treat me so!
I, the mind of the past, to be driven under the ground
out cast, like dirt!
The wind I breathe is fury and utter hate.
Earth, ah, earth
what is this agony that crawls under my ribs?
Night, hear me, o Night,

mother. They have wiped me out
and the hard hands of the gods
and their treacheries have taken my old rights away.

ATHENE

I will bear your angers. You are elder born than I
and in that you are wiser far than I. Yet still
Zeus gave me too intelligence not to be despised.
If you go away into some land of foreigners,
I warn you, you will come to love this country. Time
in his forward flood shall ever grow more dignified
for the people of this city. And you, in your place
of eminence beside Erechtheus in his house
shall win from female and from male processionals
more than all lands of men beside could ever give.
Only in this place that I haunt do not inflict
your bloody stimulus to twist the inward hearts
of young men, raging in a fury not of wine,
nor, as if plucking the heart from fighting cocks,
engraft among my citizens that spirit of war
that turns their battle fury inward on themselves.
No, let our wars range outward hard against the man
who has fallen horribly in love with high renown.
No true fighter I call the bird that fights at home.
Such life I offer you, and it is yours to take.
Do good, receive good, and be honored as the good
are honored. Share our country, the beloved of god.

CHORUS

That they could treat me so!
I, the mind of the past, to be driven under the ground
out cast, like dirt!

The wind I breathe is fury and utter hate.
Earth, ah, earth
what is this agony that crawls under my ribs?
Night, hear me, o Night,
mother. They have wiped me out
and the hard hands of the gods
and their treacheries have taken my old rights away.

ATHENE

I will not weary of telling you all the good things
I offer, so that you can never say that you,
an elder god, were driven unfriended from the land
by me in my youth, and by my mortal citizens.
But if you hold Persuasion has her sacred place
of worship, in the sweet beguilement of my voice,
then you might stay with us. But if you wish to stay
then it would not be justice to inflict your rage
upon this city, your resentment or bad luck
to armies. Yours the baron's portion in this land
if you will, in all justice, with full privilege.

CHORUS

Lady Athene, what is this place you say is mine?

ATHENE

A place free of all grief and pain. Take it for yours.

CHORUS

If I do take it, shall I have some definite powers?

ATHENE

No household shall be prosperous without your will.

CHORUS

You will do this? You will really let me be so strong?

ATHENE

So we shall straighten the lives of all who worship us.

CHORUS

You guarantee such honor for the rest of time?

ATHENE

I have no need to promise what I can not do.

CHORUS

I think you will have your way with me. My hate is
going.

ATHENE

Stay here, then. You will win the hearts of others, too.

CHORUS

I will put a spell upon the land. What shall it be?

ATHENE

Something that has no traffic with evil success.
Let it come out of the ground, out of the sea's water,
and from the high air make the waft of gentle gales
wash over the country in full sunlight, and the seed
and stream of the soil's yield and of the grazing beasts
be strong and never fail our people as time goes,
and make the human seed be kept alive. Make more
the issue of those who worship more your ways, for as
the gardener works in love, so love I best of all
the unblighted generation of these upright men.

All such is yours for granting. In the speech and show
and pride of battle, I myself shall not endure
this city's eclipse in the estimation of mankind.

CHORUS

I accept this home at Athene's side.
I shall not forget the cause
of this city, which Zeus all powerful and Ares
rule, stronghold of divinities,
glory of Hellene gods, their guarded altar.
So with forecast of good
I speak this prayer for them
that the sun's bright magnificence shall break out wave
on wave of all the happiness
life can give, across their land.

ATHENE

Here are my actions. In all good will
toward these citizens I establish in power
spirits who are large, difficult to soften.
To them is given the handling entire
of men's lives. That man
who has not felt the weight of their hands
takes the strokes of life, knows not whence, not why,
for crimes wreaked in past generations
drag him before these powers. Loud his voice
but the silent doom
hates hard, and breaks him to dust.

CHORUS

Let there blow no wind that wrecks the trees.
I pronounce words of grace.

Nor blaze of heat blind the blossoms of grown plants,
  nor
cross the circles of its right
place. Let no barren deadly sickness creep and kill.
Flocks fatten. Earth be kind
to them, with double fold of fruit
in time appointed for its yielding. Secret child
of earth, her hidden wealth, bestow
blessing and surprise of gods.

ATHENE

Strong guard of our city, hear you these
and what they portend? Fury is a high queen
of strength even among the immortal gods
and the undergods, and for humankind
their work is accomplished, absolute, clear:
for some, singing; for some, life dimmed
in tears; theirs the disposition.

CHORUS

Death of manhood cut down
before its prime I forbid:
girls' grace and glory find
men to live life with them.
Grant, you who have the power.
And o, steering spirits of law,
goddesses of destiny,
sisters from my mother, hear;
in all houses implicate,
in all time heavy of hand

on whom your just arrest befalls,
august among goddesses, bestow.

ATHENE

It is my glory to hear how these
generosities
are given my land. I admire the eyes
of Persuasion, who guided the speech of my mouth
toward these, when they were reluctant and wild.
Zeus, who guides men's speech in councils, was too
strong; and my ambition
for good wins out in the whole issue.

CHORUS

This my prayer: Civil War
fattening on men's ruin shall
not thunder in our city. Let
not the dry dust that drinks
the black blood of citizens
through passion for revenge
and bloodshed for bloodshed
be given our state to prey upon.
Let them render grace for grace.
Let love be their common will;
let them hate with single heart.
Much wrong in the world thereby is healed.

ATHENE

Are they taking thought to discover that road
where speech goes straight?
In the terror upon the faces of these

I see great good for our citizens.
While with good will you hold in high honor
these spirits, their will shall be good, as you steer
your city, your land
on an upright course clear through to the end.

CHORUS

Farewell, farewell. High destiny shall be yours
by right. Farewell, citizens
seated near the throne of Zeus,
beloved by the maiden he loves,
civilized as years go by,
sheltered under Athene's wings,
grand even in her father's sight.

ATHENE

Goddesses, farewell. Mine to lead, as these
attend us, to where
by the sacred light new chambers are given.
Go then. Sped by majestic sacrifice
from these, plunge beneath the ground. There hold
off what might hurt the land; pour in
the city's advantage, success in the end.
You, children of Cranaus, you who keep
the citadel, guide these guests of the state.
For good things given,
your hearts' desire be for good to return.

CHORUS

Farewell and again farewell, words spoken twice over,
all who by this citadel,

mortal men, spirits divine,
hold the city of Pallas, grace
this my guestship in your land.
Life will give you no regrets.

ATHENE

Well said. I assent to all the burden of your prayers,
and by the light of flaring torches now attend
your passage to the deep and subterranean hold,
as by us walk those women whose high privilege
it is to guard my image. Flower of all the land
of Theseus, let them issue now, grave companies,
maidens, wives, elder women, in processional.
In the investiture of purple stained robes
dignify them, and let the torchlight go before
so that the kindly company of these within
our ground may shine in the future of strong men to
      come.

CHORUS [by the women who have been forming for
          processional]

Home, home, o high, o aspiring
Daughters of Night, aged children, in blithe
      processional.
Bless them, all here, with silence.

In the primeval dark of earth-hollows
held in high veneration with rights sacrificial
bless them, all people, with silence.

Gracious be, wish what the land wishes,
follow, grave goddesses, flushed in the flamesprung
torchlight gay on your journey.
Singing all follow our footsteps.

There shall be peace forever between these people
of Pallas and their guests. Zeus the all seeing
met with Destiny to confirm it.
Singing all follow our footsteps.

[*Exeunt omnes, in procession.*]